The Selection and Removal of Arbitrators in Investor-State Dispute Settlement

International Investment Law and Arbitration

Volumes published in this Brill Research Perspectives title are listed at *brill.com/rpia*

The Selection and Removal of Arbitrators in Investor-State Dispute Settlement

By

Chiara Giorgetti

BRILL

LEIDEN | BOSTON

This paperback book edition is simultaneously published as issue 2.4 of *International Investment Law and Arbitration*, DOI:10.1163/24055778-12340007.

Library of Congress Control Number: 2019948638

Typeface for the Latin, Greek, and Cyrillic scripts: "Brill". See and download: brill.com/brill-typeface.

ISBN 978-90-04-41622-2 (paperback)
ISBN 978-90-04-41623-9 (e-book)

This book is printed on acid-free paper and produced in a sustainable manner.

Contents

Selecting and Removing Arbitrators in International Investment Arbitration

Chiara Giorgetti
Richmond Law School
cgiorget@richmond.edu

Abstract

This book explores and assesses two essential features in investor state dispute resolution (ISDS): the selection and the removal of arbitrators. Both topics have received increasing scrutiny and criticism, that have in turn generated calls for reforms. In its first part, this book explains the selection of arbitrators procedurally and comparatively under the most-often used arbitration rules. It then reviews critically the necessary and desirable qualities for arbitrators' selection and appointment, and addresses some important and related policy issues, such diversity and repeat appointments. Finally, it discusses the recent calls to review the methodologies used to appoint arbitrators, and specifically the proposal by the European Commission to create a permanent tribunal to resolve international investment disputes, the UNCITRAL Working Group III Reform Process and the rules amendment proposal undertaken by the Secretariat of the International Center for Settlement of Investment Disputes (ICSID Secretariat). In its second part, the book addresses the companion and similarly important issue of challenging and removing arbitrators. It does so by reviewing first the provisions that are appplied under a variety of arbitration rules to remove arbitrators who fail to possess the necessary qualities to sit in arbitral proceedings. It then evaluates the reasons for challenge and discusses some important cases that addressed challenges. The book assesses appointments and removals in a multifaceted and comprehensive way, and includes a critical assessment of the reasons and calls for reform of the ISDS system.

Keywords

Selection of Arbitrators – International Investment Arbitration – investor state dispute resolution (ISDS) – ISDS Reform – appointment of arbitrators – removal of arbitrators – recusal of arbitrators – independence and impartiality – qualities required to sit as arbitrators – party-appointment in ISDS – third-party appointment – neutral

 | DOI:10.1163/9789004416239_002

authority – Secretariat of the International Center for Settlement of Investment Disputes – ICSID – UNCITRAL – permanent investment court

Author Biography and Acknowledgments

Chiara Giorgetti is Professor of Law, Richmond Law School, JSD (Yale), LLM (Yale), MSc (LSE) Laurea (Bologna). Former Associate, White & Case, Arbitration Group and Lalive. Clerk, International Court of Justice. Admitted to the Bar in New York and D.C. The author wishes to thank Ben Midas for his excellent research assistance, Maureen Moran for her essential help finalzing this project, and Abigail J. Parsons for outstanding editorial assistance.

1 Introduction: International Investment Arbitration as a Unique Dispute Resolution Mechanism

The selection and removal of arbitrators in international investment arbitration, the two topics explored in this book,[1] are particularly salient issues in the field: they are increasingly under scrutiny and have mustered considerable interest.[2]

International investment arbitration is and remains a distinctive dispute resolution system which is rooted in public international law and also adopts procedures that are taken *mutatis mutandis* from international commercial arbitration.

Uniquely, investment arbitration addresses disputes between a foreign private investor and a sovereign state.[3] This characteristic is consequential and

1 This article builds on and updates my previous publications on these issues, namely: *Who Decides Who Decides in International Investment Arbitration?*, 35 U. Pa. J. Int'l L. 101 (2014); *Between Legitimacy and Control: Challenges and Recusals of Arbitrators and Judges in International Courts and Tribunals*, 49 Geo. Wash. Int'l Rev. 101 (2016) and *The Arbitral Tribunal: Selection and Replacement of Arbitrators*, in Litigating International Investment Disputes (C. Giorgetti ed.) (Nijhoff /Brill Publisher, 2014).

2 For example, at a recent meeting of the UNCITRAL Working Group III which focused on Investor-State Dispute Settlement Reform, delegates identified the selection and appointment of adjudicators as one of the topics for further study, see A/CN.9/970—Report of Working Group III (Investor-State Dispute Settlement Reform) on the work of its thirty-seventh session (*advance copy*), 37th Session 1–5 April 2019, available here: https://uncitral.un.org/en/working_groups/3/investor-state.

3 For a short overview, *see generally* C. Giorgetti, The Rules, Practice and Jurisprudence of International Courts and Tribunals (2012) and especially the chapters by

makes international investment arbitration a unique and hybrid dispute resolution mechanism both in terms of the substantive law it applies, which can include issues of State responsibility, treaty law and explores the regulatory powers of the State; and also in terms of procedural law, which takes much from the example of international commercial arbitration. Notably, most international investment disputes arise under bilateral investment treaties (BIT) which are governed by public international law and are concluded between two sovereign States and which empower nationals of those States with the unique ability to initiate arbitration against a foreign (host) State.[4] The investment arbitration itself is in fact between an investor and a State, though the investor is—necessarily—not party to the BIT.[5] Less often, investment arbitration cases also arise from contract or from domestic legislation.[6]

As a dispute resolution mechanism, international investment arbitration seeks to create a neutral forum to arbitrate disputes between foreign investors

---

Brooks W. Daly on the Permanent Court of Arbitration and by Carolyn Lamm et al. on the *International Center for the Settlement of Investment Disputes*. See also Christopher Schreuer et al., THE ICSID CONVENTION—A COMMENTARY (2009), Abby Cohen Smutny, *ICSID Arbitration: Procedural Review*, 2 TRANSNAT'L DISP. MGMT. 35 (2005) (discussing the proliferation of bilateral and multilateral investment treaties which provides a forum to settle disputes). Christoph Schreuer, *The Development of International Law by ICSID Tribunals*, 31(3) FOREIGN INVESTMENT LAW JOURNAL 728 (2016); MEG KINNEAR ET. AL., BUILDING INTERNATIONAL INVESTMENT LAW – THE FIRST 50 YEARS OF ICSID (2016) and CHRISTOPHER SCHREUER AND RUDOLPH DOLZER, PRINCIPLES OF INTERNATIONAL INVESTMENT LAW (2008). For an historical perspective, see TAYLOR ST JOHN, THE RISE OF INVESTOR-STATE ARBITRATION (2018).

4 Roberts refers to it as a platypus and argues that understanding the investment treaty system is difficult as "investment treaties are creature of public international law: they are entered into by one or more states and are substantively governed by public international law. However, they are distinct from most public international law because the vast majority permits investors to bring arbitral claims directly against host states based on procedural rules and enforcement mechanisms developed largely in the context of international commercial arbitration and investor-state contracts, accordingly, the system grafts private international law disputes resolutions mechanisms onto public international law treaties." Anthea Roberts, *Clash of Paradigms: Actors and Analogies Shaping the Investment Treaty System*, 107 AM. J. INT'L L. 45. *See also* Zachary Douglas, *The Hybrid Foundations of Investment Treaty Arbitration*, 2003 BRIT. Y.B. INT'L L. 151, and Zachary Douglas, *The International Law of Investment Claims* 6–10 (2009). For an overview of historical precedents of investor-state arbitration, see also Barton Legum, *The Innovation of Investor-State Arbitration Under NAFTA*, 43 HARV. J. INT'L L. 531 (2002).

5 Ian Paulsson refers to this situation as "arbitration without privity", *see* Jan Paulsson, *Arbitration Without Privity*, ICSID REV—FOREIGN INVESTMENT LAW *Journal*, Volume 10, Issue 2, Fall 1995, p. 232.

6 *See, e.g.*, James Crawford, *Treaty and Contract in Investment Arbitration*, 24 ARB INT'L 351.

and host States[7] and to provide an impartial and reliable dispute resolution system outside the national courts of either of the parties involved.[8] Indeed, one of the system's peculiar features is that the parties involved in the case are largely in charge of selecting who decides their dispute.[9]

Who selects international arbitrators and how they are selected are key elements of the system. Similarly, who is selected is also particularly relevant and has recently been the focus of much scrutiny that goes to the core of the investor-State dispute settlement (ISDS) system: how can we ensure that the selected arbitrators are and remain independent and impartial? Are arbitrators sufficiently diverse? Is the system of party-appointment appropriate for the kinds of disputes that investment arbitration resolves?[10]

This book focuses first on who selects arbitrators under the most-often used applicable rules. It then addresses the issues of the necessary and desirable qualities needed to be selected and appointed as arbitrators. Because of recent proposals and changes to the methodologies used to appoint arbitrators, a section of this book will explore the proposal by the European Commission to create a permanent tribunal to resolve international investment disputes, and the rules amendment proposal undertaken by the Secretariat of the International Center for Settlement of Investment Disputes (ICSID Secretariat) as of April 2019. The book's final section explores the companion yet opposite issue of the applicable provisions to remove and recuse an

---

7 SCHREUER ET AL., THE ICSID Convention, supra footnote 2, at 788 ("International arbitration provides an attractive alternative to the settlement of investment disputes by national courts or through diplomatic protection. Arbitration offers the parties the opportunity to select arbitrators who enjoy their confidence and who have the necessary expertise in the field. The private nature of the arbitration, assuring the confidentiality of proceedings, is often valued by parties to major economic development projects, although recently there have been calls for more transparency in international arbitration.").

8 W. Michael Reisman, *International Arbitration and Sovereignty*, 18 ARB. INT'L. 231, 235 (2002) ("The private actor is generally unwilling to subject itself to the jurisdiction of the courts in command economies or economies in transition and even when a local judiciary can boast a decree of independence, the prudent foreign investor will be alert to subtle factors that could predispose a national court in favor of the home-town team. For its part, the government that hosts an international transaction or is a party to it is, ordinarily, unwilling to subject itself to the jurisdiction of the national courts of the foreign investor.").

9 *See* C. Giorgetti, *Who Decides Who Decides in International Investment Arbitration?, supra* note 1; *See also* Andreas F. Lowenfeld, *The Party-Appointed Arbitrator in International Controversies: Some Reflections*, 30 TEX. INT'L L. J. 59, 70 (1995).

10 United Nations Commission on International Trade Law Working Group III (Investor-State Dispute Settlement Reform), Possible Reform of Investor-State Dispute Settlement (ISDS) U.N. Doc. A/CN.9/WG.III/WP.149 (September 5, 2018).

arbitrator who has lost or fails to possess the necessary qualities to sit in arbitral proceedings.

2 The Selection of Arbitrators in International Investment Arbitration

The great majority of international investment arbitrations are decided by a three-member arbitral panel, where each party selects one arbitrator, and the presiding arbitrator is selected either by agreement of the parties, the party-appointed arbitrators, or, more often, by a neutral appointing authority.[11] Their selection is not only a characteristic feature of international investment arbitration, and arbitration more generally, but also one of the most important and delicate acts taken by the parties during the proceedings.[12] Indeed, as frequent arbitrator and professor William W. Park noted, while "in real estate the three key elements are 'location, location, location,' ... in arbitration the applicable trinity is 'arbitrator, arbitrator, arbitrator'."[13]

The selection of arbitrators is made after thoughtful and in-depth research by counsel, in consultation with their client.[14] It is essential that parties nominate arbitrators who are knowledgeable, capable, and can work together. There is a lot at stake: the qualifications and arbitral skills of the arbitrators can have a significant impact on the conduct and development of the arbitration and, ultimately, on the award and its enforcement.[15] Arbitrators are the adjudicators of the dispute between the parties that has been referred to arbitration,

11 *See generally* C. Giorgetti, *Who Decides Who Decides in International Investment Arbitration?, supra* note 1.

12 *See* Constantine Partasides, *The Selection, Appointment and Challenge of Arbitrators*, 5 VINDABONA J. 217, 217 (2001) (observing that the ability of the parties to influence the composition of the arbitral tribunal is one of the defining aspects of the arbitral process and that "their power to appoint, and the power to challenge, arbitrators are two of their most powerful tools").

13 As quoted in *Kluwer Arbitration Blog*, "The International Arbitrator Information Project: An Idea Whose Time Has Come," post authored by Catherine Rogers, Aug. 9, 2012, *available at* Kluwerarbitrationblog.org.

14 Michael Waibel & Yanhui Wu, *Are Arbitrators Political?, ASIL* Research Forum 13 (Nov. 5, 2011) (noting that "the parties to investment arbitration cases and especially their counsel spend a great deal of time and effort to scrutinize the backgrounds of arbitrators, their relationship with the parties, published works and prior appointments. The time spent on choosing the right arbitrators suggests that the personality and background of the arbitrators matters substantially for arbitration outcomes.").

15 Wendy Miles, *International Arbitrator Appointment*, 57 DISP. RESOL. J. 36 (2002).

and they are ultimately empowered to render a final and binding award on the parties. During the course of the proceedings, they will have the power to decide both substantive and procedural issues relevant to the parties' dispute. The quality of the arbitrators is essential for a successful arbitration and, more generally, for the reputation of the arbitration process itself.

The section below describes the process for the selection of arbitrators, by describing first how they are selected, and then by focusing on the necessary and desirable qualities an arbitrator should possess.

3 The Procedure: Who Selects and Appoints Arbitrators?

The selection and appointment of arbitrators to international tribunals involves multiple steps, which depend on the applicable consent instrument and the institutional rules applicable to the dispute.[16] The specific applicable procedures are found in the relevant dispute resolution instrument on which the parties rely to bring the case, most often the applicable BIT or a regional investment and trade agreement in force between the State that received the investment (host state) and the state of which the investor is a national (home state).[17] Consent to arbitration can also be incorporated in contracts between the State and the investor or in national law. The dispute resolution clauses included in these instruments also specify the applicable rules.

In most cases, each party in the dispute selects at least one arbitrator. A neutral appointing authority selects the third arbitrator, who presides over the dispute, and also makes any default appointments.

Dispute resolution instruments generally provide for arbitration either under the Convention on the Settlement of Investment Disputes between States and Nationals of other States (ICSID Convention), or under the Arbitration Rules of the United Nations Commission on International Trade Law (UNCITRAL

16 For an excellent discussion on the selection process at the International Court of Justice and the International Criminal Court, *see generally* RUTH MACKENZIE, ET AL., SELECTING INTERNATIONAL JUDGES—PRINCIPLES, PROCESS AND POLITICS, (Oxford 2010).

17 More rarely, a contract or national investment law may also provide for international investment arbitration as an option. *See* International Centre for Settlement of Investment Disputes, 2013–1 ICSID CASELOAD STATISTICS 1, 7 (2013), *available at* https://icsid.worldbank.org/ICSID/FrontServlet?requestType=ICSIDDocRH&actionVal=ShowDocument&CaseLoadStatistics=True&language=English41 (graphically indicating the number of cases registered in a calendar year).

Arbitration Rules).[18] For example, the 2012 US Model BIT explains that claimants can submit their claims under the ICSID Convention and Rules, the ICSID Additional Facility Rules, or the UNCITRAL Arbitration Rules.[19]

---

18 *See* International Centre for Settlement of Investment Disputes, ICSID Convention, Regulations and Rules, Rules of Procedure for Arbitration Proceedings (Arbitration Rules), 99 (2006), available at https://icsid.worldbank.org/en/documents/icsiddocs/icsid%20convention%20english.pdf [hereinafter ICSID Convention and ICSID Rules]; ICSID Convention (amended 2006); UNCITRAL Arbitration Rules as revised in 2010, G.A. Res. 65/22, U.N. DOC. A/RES/65/22 (Jan. 10, 2010) [hereinafter UNCITRAL Arbitration Rules (2010)]. Conclusions reached analyzing their practice, therefore, provide generally applicable lessons.

19 U.S. MODEL BIT, art. 24(3)(2012), *available at* http://www.state.gov/e/eb/ifd/bit/index.htm (indicating that "Provided that six months have elapsed since the events giving rise to the claim, a claimant may submit a claim referred to in para. 1: a. Under the ICSID Convention and the ICSID Rules of Procedure for Arbitration Proceedings, provided that both respondent and the non-disputing Party are parties to the ICSID Convention; b. Under the ICSID Additional Facility Rules, provided that either the respondent or the non-disputing party is a party to the ICSID Convention; c. Under the UNCITRAL Arbitration Rules; or d. If the claimant and respondent agree, to any other arbitration institution or under any other arbitration rules"). Similarly, Chapter Eleven of the North American Free Trade Agreement (NAFTA) contains provisions related to the settlement of disputes related to cross-borders investors and provides that investors can submit their claims under the ICSID Convention, the ICSID Additional Facility Rules or under the UNCITRAL Arbitration Rules. North American Free Trade Agreement (NAFTA) art. 1120, December 17,1992, 32 I.L.M.289, *available at* http://www.nafta-alena.gc.ca/en/view.aspx?x=299&mtpiID=142#A1125 (indicating that "[e]xcept as provided in Annex 1120.1, and provided that six months have elapsed since the events giving rise to a claim, a disputing investor may submit the claim to arbitration under: (a) the ICSID Convention, provided that both the disputing Party and the Party of the investor are parties to the Convention; (b) the Additional Facility Rules of ICSID, provided that either the disputing Party or the Party of the investor, but not both, is a party to the ICSID Convention; or (c) the UNCITRAL Arbitration Rules"). Other rules complete the procedural framework applicable to ICSID disputes, including the ICSID Rules for Arbitration Proceedings, the Administrative and Financial Regulations, the Rules of Procedure for the Institution of Conciliation and Arbitration Proceedings and the Additional Facility Rules. These rules can be found on the website of ICSID, at: https://icsid.worldbank.org/ICSID/ICSID/RulesMain.jsp. UNCITRAL rules can be found on the PCA website at: http://pca-cpa.org/shownews.asp?ac=actual&pag_id=1261. Similarly, the Permanent Court of Arbitration also provides for additional and more specific rules. In December 2012, the Administrative Council of the PCA adopted a new set of procedural rules, the "PCA Arbitration Rules 2012," for the arbitration of disputes involving at least one State, a State-controlled entity, or an international organization, which consolidate previous rules of procedures. The new Rules are available at http://www.pca-cpa.org/showpage.asp?pag_id=1188. They are a consolidation of four sets of PCA procedural rules from the 1990s—the Optional Rules for Arbitrating Disputes between Two States (1992), the Optional Rules for Arbitrating Disputes between Two Parties of Which Only One is a State (1993), the Optional Rules

Other rules of procedures that are used, albeit less frequently, in investment arbitration are those of the London Court of International Arbitration (LCIA), the International Chamber of Commerce (ICC), the Arbitration Institute of the Stockholm Chamber of Commerce (SCC), and the rules developed by the Permanent Court of Arbitration (PCA).[20]

Table 1 in the appendix summarizes the applicable rules, including default rules which apply if one of the parties do not agree or if one of the parties fail to nominate its arbitrators.

3.1 *Party Appointments*

In most cases, each party in the dispute selects at least one arbitrator. This gives the parties substantial say on the persons selected to judge their case, and it is one of the most important features of international arbitration, including commercial arbitration, investment arbitration, or inter-State arbitrations.[21] As one commentator notes, "the selection of the party-appointed arbitrator may be the most critical decision in an international arbitral proceeding."[22]

---

for Arbitration Between International Organizations and States (1996), and the Optional Rules for Arbitration Between International Organizations and Private Parties (1996).

20 London Court of International Arbitration, (Oct. 1, 2014), available at http://www.lcia.org/dispute_resolution_services/lcia-arbitration-rules-2014.aspx [hereinafter LCIA Arbitration Rules 2014]; International Chamber of Commerce Rules of Arbitration, (Mar. 1, 2017), available at https://cdn.iccwbo.org/content/uploads/sites/3/2017/01/ICC-2017-Arbitration-and-2014-Mediation-Rules-english-version.pdf.pdf [hereinafter ICC Arbitration Rules 2017]; Arbitration Rules of the Arbitration Institute of the Stockholm Chamber of Commerce, (Jan 1, 2017), available at https://sccinstitute.com/media/293614/arbitration_rules_eng_17_web.pdf [hereinafter SCC Arbitration Rules 2017]; Permanent Court of Arbitration—Arbitration Rules 2012, (Dec. 17, 2012), available at https://pca-cpa.org/wp-content/uploads/sites/175/2015/11/PCA-Arbitration-Rules-2012.pdf [hereinafter PCA Arbitration Rules 2012].

21 *See generally* C. Giorgetti, *Who Decides Who Decides in International Investment Arbitration?*, *supra* note 1. *See also* Andreas Lowenfeld, *The Party-Appointed Arbitrator in International Controversies: Some Reflections*, 30 TEXAS INT'L L. J. 59 (1995); James Wangelin, *Effective Selection of Arbitrators in International Arbitration*, 14 MEALEY'S INT'L ARB. REP. 69 (Nov. 1999); R. Doak Bishop & Lucy Reed, *Practical Guidelines for Interviewing, Selecting and Challenging Party-Appointed Arbitrators in International Commercial Arbitration*, 14 ARB. INT'L 395 (1998); Partasides, *The Selection, Appointment and Challenge of Arbitrators*, *supra* note 12; Wendy Miles, *International Arbitrator Appointment*, *supra* note 15.

22 Wendy Miles notes that "the constitution of the arbitral tribunal is one of the most important steps in an international arbitration. The skills and qualifications of the arbitrators and the number of members on the tribunal may have significant impact on the development of the dispute resolution and, ultimately, the award itself." *See* Wendy Miles, *International Arbitrator Appointment*, *supra* note 15, at 36.

The dispute resolution clause of most BITs typically provides for the arbitrator selection method to be adopted in the proceedings. For example, the 2012 U.S. Model BIT provides that, unless otherwise agreed by the disputing parties, "the tribunal shall comprise three arbitrators, one arbitrator appointed by each of the disputing parties and the third, who shall be the presiding arbitrator, appointed by agreement of the disputing parties."[23]

In the absence of choice, the ICSID Convention also contains default rules. Under ICSID, the arbitral Tribunal "shall consist of three arbitrators, one arbitrator appointed by each party and the third, who shall be the president of the Tribunal, appointed by agreement of the parties."[24] Under ICSID proceedings, Arbitration Rule 3 specifies that in a communication to the other party, a party names two persons, identifying one of them "as the arbitrator appointed by it, and the other as the arbitrator proposed to be the President of the Tribunal" and invites the other party to concur in the appointment of the arbitrator proposed to be the President of the Tribunal and to appoint another arbitrator." Upon receipt, the other party promptly replies by naming a person appointed by it and either concurs on the appointment of the President or names another person as the proposed arbitrator. The initiating party then notifies the other party if they concur with the choice of President.[25] Parties themselves select

23 U.S. Model BIT, Art. 27 (Selection of arbitrators). Likewise, NAFTA Art. 1123 provides for the number of arbitrators and method of appointment and explains that "unless the disputing parties otherwise agree, the Tribunal shall comprise three arbitrators, one arbitrator appointed by each of the disputing parties and the third, who shall be the presiding arbitrator, appointed by agreement of the disputing parties." NAFTA, Art. 1123 (Number of Arbitrators and Method of Appointment).

24 ICSID Rules, *supra* note 18, Art. 37; *accord* UNCITRAL Rules (1976), Art. 5 ("If the parties have not previously agreed on the number of arbitrators (i.e. one or three), and if within fifteen days after the receipt by the respondent of the notice of arbitration the parties have not agreed that there shall be only one arbitrator, three arbitrators shall be appointed.").

25 ICSID Arbitration Rule 3 (Appointment of Arbitrators to a Tribunal Constituted in Accordance with Convention Article 37(2)(b)) provides that "(1) If the Tribunal is to be constituted in accordance with Article 37(2)(b) of the Convention: (a) either party shall in a communication to the other party: (i) name two persons, identifying one of them, who shall not have the same nationality as nor be a national of either party, as the arbitrator appointed by it, and the other as the arbitrator proposed to be the President of the Tribunal; and (ii) invite the other party to concur in the appointment of the arbitrator proposed to be the President of the Tribunal and to appoint another arbitrator; (b) promptly upon receipt of this communication the other party shall, in its reply: (i) name a person as the arbitrator appointed by it, who shall not have the same nationality as nor be a national of either party; and (ii) concur in the appointment of the arbitrator proposed to be the President of the Tribunal or name another person as the arbitrator proposed to be President; (c) promptly upon receipt of the reply containing such a proposal, the

their arbitrators in the majority of cases, in sixty-five percent of the time in the case of ICSID.[26] Acceptance of the claimant's proposal for the presiding or sole arbitrator by respondent is rare, however, and that appointment is normally negotiated by the parties together over several weeks and often finally decided by a third party, such as an appointing authority.

The UNCITRAL Rules similarly provide that "[i]f three arbitrators are to be appointed, each party shall appoint one arbitrator. The two arbitrators thus appointed shall choose the third arbitrator who will act as the presiding arbitrator of the arbitral tribunal."[27] The claimant includes a notification of the appointment of its arbitrator in the notice of arbitration sent to the respondent which is the initial act of the arbitration.[28]

The Rules of the International Chamber of Commerce (ICC) are slightly different and provide for a sole arbitrator as the default choice. Article 12 provides that if the parties have not agreed on the number of arbitrators, the International Court of Arbitration of the ICC (the Court) appoints a sole arbitrator.[29] This choice is easily justified by the variety of cases, including small commercial cases, which are resolved using the ICC Rules. However, when the Court considers that the dispute "is such as to warrant the appointment of three arbitrators" the procedure is similar to that of other investment arbitration rules.[30] In such cases, the claimant nominates "an arbitrator within a period

---

initiating party shall notify the other party whether it concurs in the appointment of the arbitrator proposed by that party to be the President of the Tribunal. (2) The communications provided for in this Rule shall be made or promptly confirmed in writing and shall either be transmitted through the Secretary-General or directly between the parties with a copy to the Secretary-General."

26 Eloïse M. Obadia, *Remarks at 105th ASIL Annual Meeting*, 105 ASIL ANN. MTG. PROC. 74 (2011). Historically, of the total 850 appointments made by ICSID in cases registered under the ICSID Convention and Additional Facility since its first case, 460 were made by parties. In 2012, party-appointed arbitrators counted for 101 of the 139 appointments, in ICSID, THE ICSID CASELOAD—STATISTICS 2012, at19, 31 (2012). More recent statistics show that 65% of appointment are made by the parties at ICSID, *see* International Centre for Settlement of Investment Disputes, ICSID Annual Report 1, 32 (2018), available at https://icsid.worldbank.org/en/Documents/resources/2018ICSIDAnnualReport.ENG.pdf.

27 UNCITRAL Rule (2010), Art. 9; *see also* UNCITRAL Rule (1976), Art. 7. The full text of the Rules can be found on the website of the Permanent Court of Arbitration at http://PCA-CPA.org/showpage.asp?pag_id=1064.

28 *Id.* UNCITRAL Rule (2010), Art. 3.

29 ICC Rules 2012, Art. 12(2), *available at* http://www.iccwbo.org/. Note that the Court is the independent arbitration body of the ICC, and despite the name it does not itself resolve disputes. Its role is limited to administrating the resolution of disputes by the arbitral tribunals. *See* ICC Rules, Art. 1.

30 *Id.*

of 15 days from the receipt of the notification of the decision of the Court, and the respondent shall nominate an arbitrator within a period of 15 days from the receipt of the notification of the nomination made by the claimant." Importantly, the Court needs to confirm the nominations of the arbitrators.[31]

Under the PCA Rules, the parties have a choice of a sole arbitrator, three or five arbitrators. Unless the parties have agreed on the number of arbitrators previously, and if within 30 days after the receipt by the respondent of the notice of arbitration the parties have not agreed on the number of arbitrators, three arbitrators are to be appointed.[32] If three arbitrators are to be appointed, each party appoints one arbitrator, and then these two arbitrators choose the third who will act as the presiding arbitrator.[33] If five arbitrators are to be appointed, each party appoints one arbitrator, and then these two arbitrators choose the remaining three arbitrators, one of whom the party-appointed arbitrators designate as the presiding arbitrator.[34]

Under the Rules of the SCC, the parties may agree on the number of arbitrators and if they fail to do so, the Board of Directors of the SCC ("the Board") decides whether the tribunal should be composed of a sole arbitrator or three arbitrators.[35] Parties may agree on the procedure for appointing the tribunal, and if they do not, then the Board decides. If the parties decide to appoint more than one arbitrator, each party appoints an equal number of arbitrators and the Board appoints a chairperson. If there are multiple claimants or multiple respondents and the tribunal is to consist of more than one arbitrator, the multiple claimants jointly and the multiple respondents jointly appoint an equal number of arbitrators.[36]

Under the LCIA Rules, parties may agree to nominate arbitrators as they prefer, but the appointment itself is done by the LCIA Court.[37] If the parties do not make their nomination in time, the LCIA Court appoints the missing arbitrators.

3.2 *Non-Party Appointments*

In addition to one party appointments, at least one arbitrator—the President or the sole arbitrator—is selected by agreement of the parties or by a neutral authority. A neutral authority usually plays a role in arbitrator selection under

31 *Id.* ICC Rules, Art. 1(2).
32 PCA Arbitration Rules Art. 7(1).
33 PCA Arbitration Rules Art. 9(1).
34 PCA Arbitration Rules Art. 9(1).
35 SCC Rules, Article 16.
36 SCC Rules, Article 17.
37 LCIA, Art. 7.

most applicable rules. The neutral appointing authority selects an arbitrator when there is no agreement among the parties on the selection of the president of the arbitral tribunal, or when one of the parties defaults in its selection.

3.2.1 International Convention on the Settlement of Investment Disputes

In ICSID proceedings, if the respondent defaults the Chairperson of ICSID's Administrative Council, who is also the President of the World Bank, appoints the missing arbitrators.[38] In his or her choice of arbitrators, the Chairperson of the ICSID Administrative Council is restricted to those people listed in the Panel of Arbitrators, which only includes names of arbitrators selected by ICSID Contracting Parties and by the Chairperson him or herself.[39] The same rules also apply for the selection of the Presiding and sole arbitrator.

38 ICSID Rules, *supra* note 18, Art. 38 ("If the Tribunal shall not have been constituted within 90 days after notice of registration of the request has been dispatched by the Secretary-General in accordance with paragraph (3) of Article 36, or such other period as the parties may agree, the Chairman shall, at the request of either party and after consulting both parties as far as possible, appoint the arbitrator or arbitrators not yet appointed. Arbitrators appointed by the Chairman pursuant to this Article shall not be nationals of the Contracting State party to the dispute or of the Contracting State whose national is a party to the dispute."). In practice, what happens is that once the ninety days have expired, the ICSID Secretariat would first try to find an agreement between the parties. To that end, they will first propose to the parties a roster of three persons and ask the parties to advise the Secretary General—and not each other—whether they would agree on these proposals, without explanations. If the parties agree, then the person is named and become the president of the tribunal. This result would be counted as a party-selection. *See* Eloïse M. Obadia, *Remarks at the 105th ASIL Annual Meeting,* note 26, at 76. The most recent ICSID Statistics shows that ICSID makes about 40% of arbitral appointments. The ICSID Caseload—Statistics (Issue 2018–2), p. 20 (of 1453 total appointments, ICSID appointed 589). NAFTA similarly provides that if the tribunal is not constituted within ninety days from the date of the claim submission to arbitration, the Secretary-General, on the request of either disputing party, shall appoint the arbitrators not yet appointed. NAFTA, Art. 1124(2) (providing that "If a Tribunal, other than a Tribunal established under Article 1126, has not been constituted within 90 days from the date that a claim is submitted to arbitration, the Secretary-General, on the request of either disputing party, shall appoint, in his discretion, the arbitrator or arbitrators not yet appointed, except that the presiding arbitrator shall be appointed in accordance with paragraph 3.").

39 ICSID Rules, *supra* note 18, Art. 40 ("(1) Arbitrators may be appointed from outside the Panel of Arbitrators, except in the case of appointments by the Chairman pursuant to Article 38."). Each contracting state has a right to designate up to four persons to the Panel of Arbitrators. The Chairperson of the ICSID Administrative Tribunal can designate ten persons. The appointment is for ten years, but it can continue until the nomination is expressly revoked.

The Chairperson also selects all the three members of *ad hoc* annulment committees.[40] When selecting members of *ad hoc* annulment committees, the Chairperson is also limited to nominate only members from the Panel of Arbitrators and cannot designate those nominated to the Panel of Arbitrators by either of the two states involved.[41]

To expedite the arbitrator selection process and assist the parties in identifying, if possible, a mutually acceptable candidate, the ICSID Secretariat has developed a procedure called "the ballot procedure."[42] Under this procedure, ICSID proposes to the parties three to seven candidates in a list ("ballot") and requests them to advise the Secretary-General if any of these potential appointees would be acceptable. The parties send their completed ballots to the ICSID Secretariat only, without sharing them with the other party. If this procedure results in the identification of a candidate who is mutually acceptable to both parties, that person will be appointed pursuant to the parties' agreement. If the parties agree on more than one proposed appointee, ICSID selects one of those persons and informs the parties of the selection.[43] At times, the ICSID

---

40 On annulment, see C. GIORGETTI (ED.), LITIGATING INTERNATIONAL INVESTMENT DISPUTES (2014), supra note 1, especially Chapter 16 "Post-Awards Remedies" by Heiskanen and Halone.

41 Under ICSID Convention, Article 13, each Contracting party may designate to the Panel of Arbitrators four persons, including its nationals. The Chairperson can designate ten persons, each having a different nationality. Not all contracting states have exercised their right to nominate. *See* Obadia, *supra* note 26, at 75.

42 For a more detailed description of the selection procedure by the Secretariat, see Chapter 4: "Institutional Arbitration and the Role of the Secretariat," by Obadia and Nitschke in LITIGATING INTERNATIONAL INVESTMENT DISPUTES, supra note 1. See also above section 3.1. This is technically a party-appointment, though it is lead procedurally by the Secretariat.

43 Note that the ICSID Secretariat is—at the moment of writing in 2019—undertaking an important exercise of amending its rules. If the proposed amendments are accepted by the ISCID Member States, the selection process will also change. The amendments provide for shorter timing and the facilitation of the appointment of the arbitral tribunals. Specifically, the proposed rules require parties to disclose whether they have third-party funding, the source of the funding, and to keep such disclosure of information current through the proceeding. The new proposed rules also enhance the efficiency in constitution of Tribunals. The default formula (two-party appointed arbitrators and an agreed-upon President) will apply automatically 60 days after the date of registration unless the parties advise the Secretary-General otherwise. The new proposed rules eliminate the former multi-step process for Tribunal constitution, and offers the assistance of the Secretary General in appointing the President of the Tribunal or sole arbitrator. It also allows parties to request assistance at any stage and gives them the ability to ask for different types of assistance including a (non-binding) ballot, and a (binding) list process. The

Secretariat also provides the parties with a list of possible presidents which the parties may then rank. The highest ranked person by both parties will then be appointed by the Secretariat. These 'hybrid' selection mechanisms—which include both the secretariat and the parties—helps with the timely and smooth selection of arbitrators and can also result in a tribunal that enjoys greater support of the parties.

3.2.2 United Nations Commission on International Trade Law

Under both the 1976[44] and the 2010[45] UNCITRAL Rules, parties can request the Secretary General of the PCA to designate an "appointing authority" for the purpose of appointing an arbitral tribunal if the parties fail to do so by the prescribed limit of thirty days.[46] In addition, under the 2010 UNCITRAL Rules, a party may also propose that the PCA Secretary General him or herself acts as the appointing authority.

UNCITRAL provisions also specify how the appointing authority should go about making its nomination. First, at the request of one of the parties, the appointing authority communicates to both parties an identical list containing at least three names for possible appointment as arbitrator. Second, within a specified deadline, each party returns the list to the appointing authority after deleting the names to which the party objects and numbering the remaining names on the list in the order of preference. Third, and finally, the appointing authority will select the missing arbitrators following the preferences outlined by the parties.[47] Unsurprisingly, the PCA reports that the majority of the requests to appoint respondent's arbitrators were withdrawn, and the

---

new proposed rules give appointees 20 days to accept appointment and send their declaration, instead of allowing the declaration to be filed by the first session as is currently done. They also provide for an expanded arbitrator declaration form giving more information for purposes of identifying potential conflict. *See* ICSID Secretariat, Proposals for Amendment of the ICSID Rules-Synopsis (August 2, 2018), available at https://icsid.worldbank.org/en/amendments/Documents/Homepage/Amendments-Vol_1_Synopsis_EN,FR,SP.pdf.

44 Note that under the UNCITRAL Rules, the first attempt to choose the presiding arbitrator is given to the two part-appointed arbitrators. UNCITRAL Arbitration Rules (1976), Arts. 6, 7 & 12.

45 UNCITRAL Arbitration Rules (2010), Arts. 6 & 8–13.

46 Permanent Court of Arbitration, "111th Annual Report," 1 (2011). For an interesting overview of the PCA's appointing authority activity in 2011, see *id.* at 11–13.

47 UNCITRAL Arbitration Rules (1976), Art. 7; UNCITRAL Arbitration Rules (2010), Art. 6.

selection was finally made by the party itself, once the party fully appreciated the importance of the issues at stake.[48]

3.2.3 Permanent Court of Arbitration

Under the PCA Rules, if no other parties have responded to a party's proposal to appoint a sole arbitrator within these 30 days, and the party or parties concerned have failed to appoint a second arbitrator, a party may request the appointing authority to appoint a sole arbitrator and it may do so if it determines that it is appropriate.[49] If the parties have previously agreed to appoint a sole arbitrator and did not reach an agreement within 30 days, either party may request the appointing authority to appoint a sole arbitrator.[50] As soon as possible, the appointing authority shall make the appointment using the list procedure as follows: (a) The appointing authority sends a list containing at least three names to each of the parties; (b) each party, within 15 days, may privately send the list back to the appointing authority after deleting the names to which it objects and numbering the remaining names in the order of its preference; (c) after 15 days, the appointing authority shall appoint the sole arbitrator from among the names approved on the lists returned to it and in accordance with the order of preference indicated by the parties; (d) If for any reason the appointment cannot be made according to this procedure, the appointing authority may exercise its discretion in appointing the sole arbitrator.[51] The appointing authority may determine that the list procedure is not appropriate for a specific case.[52]

If three or five arbitrators are to be appointed, each party appoints one arbitrator, and then these two arbitrators choose either the third presiding arbitrator[53] or the remaining three and designate one of these three as the presiding arbitrator.[54] If the second party fails to select the second arbitrator or notify the first party of its selection within 30 days, the first party may request

48 Permanent Court of Arbitration, "111th Annual Report," *supra* note 46, at 11–13. Note that in 2011, under the above UNCITRAL provisions, the PCA received eighteen new requests that the Secretary-General designate an appointing authority for the appointment of arbitrators and ten requests that the Secretary-General act as appointing authority for the appointment of arbitrators. Of these, eight related to the appointment of the presiding arbitrator or a sole arbitrator. *Id.*

49 PCA Arbitration Rules Art. 7(2).

50 PCA Arbitration Rules Art. 8(1).

51 PCA Arbitration Rules Art. 8(2).

52 PCA Arbitration Rules Art. 8(2).

53 PCA Arbitration Rules Art. 9(1).

54 PCA Arbitration Rules Art. 9(1).

the appointing authority to select the second arbitrator.[55] If the two arbitrators appointed by the parties fail to reach an agreement on the remaining arbitrators within 30 days, the appointment shall be made by the appointing authority.[56]

Where three or five arbitrators are to be appointed and there are multiple parties as claimant or as respondent, the multiple parties jointly, whether as claimant or as respondent, shall appoint an arbitrator unless the parties have agreed to another method.[57] If the parties have agreed that the arbitral tribunal is to be composed of a number of arbitrators other than one, three, or five, then the parties shall appoint the arbitrators as previously agreed.[58] If there was a failure to constitute the arbitral tribunal, either party may request the appointing authoring to constitute an arbitral tribunal which has the freedom to revoke previously appointed arbitrators, and designate a presiding arbitrator.[59] The parties and the appointing authority are free to choose persons who are not Members of the Permanent Court of Arbitration[60]

3.2.4 International Chamber of Commerce

Under the ICC Rules, if a dispute is referred to three arbitrators, the default rule is that the third and presiding arbitrator is appointed by the Court, unless the parties have agreed on another procedure for such appointment. If, under such procedure, the parties fail to reach an agreement within the prescribed time limit, the third arbitrator is appointed by the Court. The Court appoints the arbitrator also when a party fails to nominate one.[61] The Court confirms the Parties' nominations pursuant to Article 13 of the ICC Rules. When confirming or appointing arbitrators, the ICC Court will usually consider the nationality, residence, and other relationships that the prospective arbitrators have with the countries of which the parties or the other arbitrators are nationals, as well as the prospective arbitrator's availability and ability to conduct the arbitration in accordance with the Rules.[62] In general, when the ICC Court appoints an arbitrator, it makes the appointment based on the proposal of the ICC National Committee or Group that it considers to be appropriate.[63] If, however, the

55 PCA Arbitration Rules Art. 9(2).
56 PCA Arbitration Rules Art. 9(3).
57 PCA Arbitration Rules Art. 10(1).
58 PCA Arbitration Rules Art. 10(2).
59 PCA Arbitration Rules Art. 10(3).
60 PCA Arbitration Rules Art. 10(4).
61 ICC Rules, Art. 12.
62 ICC Rules, Art. 13 (1).
63 ICC Rules, Art. 13 (2).

Court decides not to accept the proposal made, or if the National Committee or Group fails to make the proposal requested within the prescribed time limit, the Court may repeat its request, request a proposal from another National Committee or Group that it considers to be appropriate, or appoint directly any person whom it regards as suitable.[64] When, as is the case in international investment arbitration, one of the parties is a State, the Court may also directly appoint to act as arbitrator any person whom it regards as suitable.[65]

3.2.5 Stockholm Chamber of Commerce

Under the SCC Rules, if the parties have not agreed on the number of arbitrators, the Board decides, having regards to the complexity of the case, the amount in dispute and any other relevant circumstances.[66] The parties may also decide on the procedure and timing for appointment of the Arbitral Tribunal, if the parties fail to agree, the Board decides. If the Arbitral Tribunal is to consist of a sole arbitrator, the parties are given 10 days to jointly appoint the arbitrator. If they fail to appoint the arbitrator within this time, the Board makes the appointment. If the Arbitral Tribunal is to consist of more than one arbitrator, each party appoints an equal number of arbitrators and the Board appoints the Chairperson. The Board also appoints the arbitrators whom the Parties fail to appoint within the stipulated time period. If there are multiple Claimants or Respondents and the Tribunal is to consist of more than one arbitrator, the multiple Claimants jointly and the multiple Respondents jointly appoint an equal number of arbitrators. The Board then appoints the entire Tribunal if the either side fails to appoint.[67] When appointing arbitrators, the Board should consider the nature and circumstances of the dispute, the applicable law, the seat and language of the arbitration and the nationality of the parties.[68]

3.2.6 London Court of International Arbitration

Under LCIA Rules, the LCIA Court is empowered to appoint arbitrators.[69] A sole arbitrator is appointed, unless the parties have otherwise agreed in writing or if the LCIA Court determines that in the circumstances a three-member (or, exceptionally, more than three) tribunal is appropriate.[70] The Court appoints

64 ICC Rules, Art. 13 (3).
65 ICC Rules, Art. 13 (4).
66 SCC Rules, Art. 16.
67 SCC Rules, Art. 17.
68 SCC Rules, Art. 17(7).
69 LCIA Rules, Art. 5.7.
70 LCIA Rules, Art. 5.8.

arbitrators with due regard for any particular method or criteria of selection agreed in writing by the parties.[71] The parties may also decide to nominate the arbitrators, or ask any third person to nominate them. The LCIA Court will then appoint such nominee only if that nominee provides to the Register in writing: a brief summary of his or her qualifications and professional positions, a written agreement on the fee-rates conforming with the LCIA Schedule of Costs, a signed declaration that to the candidate's best knowledge there are no circumstances that are likely to give rise in the mind of any party to any justifiable doubts about the candidate's impartiality or independence and a declaration that the candidate is ready, willing and able to devote sufficient time, diligence and industry to ensure an expeditious and efficient conduct of the proceeding.[72] The LCIA Court may refuse to appoint any nominee if it determines that the nominee has not complied with its requests or is otherwise unsuitable.[73] Similar disclosures are also required by other institutions.[74] The LCIA Court also appoints all arbitrators who are not nominated in time by the claimant, the respondent or any other third party that had the duty to nominate arbitrators.[75] When the LCIA Court appoints arbitrators, it takes into account the transaction at issue, the nature and circumstances of the dispute, its monetary amount or value, the location and languages of the parties, the number of parties and all other factors which it may consider relevant in the circumstances.[76] When there are three or more parties in an arbitration, and the parties have not agreed in writing that they represent two separate sides for the formation of the tribunal, the LCIA Court appoints the entire tribunal.[77]

Table 2 in the Appendix summarizes the provisions applicable to non-Party appointment and the obligations of appointing authorities must respect when making such appointments.

3.3 *Looking at the Future: Appointment in Permanent Courts*

As a radical alternative to the selection of arbitrators by parties or an appointing authority that has characterized investment treaty arbitration to date, recent proposals call for the creation of a permanent tribunal of sitting judges, possibly in conjunction with the creation of an appellate body

71 LCIA Rules, Art. 5.9.
72 LCIA Rules Art. 5(4) to 5(7).
73 LCIA Rules Art. 7.1.
74 See infra section 4.1.2.
75 LCIA Rules Art. 7.2.
76 LCIA Rules Art. 5.9.
77 LCIA Rules, Art. 8.

for investment arbitration. The idea of a permanent tribunal—modelled after other existing international mechanisms like the International Court of Justice—has recently become more prominent, partly as a response to criticisms of the party-selection system, and specifically as a reaction to "double-hatting" (when the same person serves both as counsel and arbitrator in different investment arbitration cases), conflicts of interest as a consequence of multiple appointments (by the same party or counsel) and the lack of diversity of the arbitrators' pool.[78] These criticisms generally concern the legitimacy of the ISDS mechanism writ large. In April 2019, UNCITRAL Working Group III embarked on a study to assess different proposal to reform the ISDS system, including the selection and appointment of arbitrators.[79]

The European Union (EU) has become the leading proponent of a permanent multilateral investment court that would replace the prevailing system of *ad hoc* investment treaty arbitration entirely. The creation of such a permanent multilateral investment court seems to be, for the moment, distant prospect. In the meantime, however, the EU has included a permanent bilateral investment court system in its most recent investment and free trade agreements, including the Comprehensive Economic and Trade Agreement between the EU and Canada (CETA),[80] the EU-Singapore Free Trade Agreement (FTA)[81] and the EU-Vietnam Free Trade Agreement.[82] At the time of writing none of these bilateral investment courts have been established: CETA is partially applied since 2017, but it does not provisionally apply the rules on the permanent court; the EU Singapore Agreement has been approved by the European

78 *See generally*, C. Giorgetti, *Who Decides Who Decides in International Investment Arbitration?*, *supra* Note 1.

79 UNCITRAL Working Group III (Investor-State Dispute Settlement Reform) discussed these issues in its April 2019 meeting, see A/CN.9/970—Report of Working Group III (Investor-State Dispute Settlement Reform) on the work of its thirty-seventh session (*advance copy*), 37th Session 1–5 April 2019, available here: https://uncitral.un.org/en/working_groups/3/investor-state. Members of the Academic Forum of the UNCITRAL Working Group III on ISDS has drafted a series of concept papers on some of the most cogent issues for discussion, including arbitration duration and cost, arbitrators' diversity and impartiality and awards consistency. A series of posts summarizing and linking the papers appeared in EJILTalk! in April 2019, available at: https://www.ejiltalk.org/reform-of-isds-matching-concerns-and-solutions/.

80 Comprehensive Economic Trade Agreement, EU-Can. (CETA) signed October 30, 2016, available at http://ec.europa.eu/trade/policy/in-focus/ceta/.

81 European Union-Singapore Free Trade Agreement, EU-Singapore, available at http://ec.europa.eu/trade/policy/countries-and-regions/countries/singapore/.

82 European Union-Vietnam Free Trade Agreement, EU-Vietnam, available at http://ec.europa.eu/trade/policy/countries-and-regions/countries/vietnam/.

Commission, and still needs to be agreed upon by the European Council and the European Parliament;[83] and the final text of the EU-Vietnam Free Trade Agreement has been finalized in July 2018, but the text awaits signature and conclusion.[84] A trade agreement "in principle" has also been reached between the EU and Mexico.[85]

The EU framework establishes a two-tiered permanent tribunal of first instance and an appellate body to resolve investment disputes between investors and host States. Chapter Eight of CETA, for example, would establish the CETA Joint Committee. The Joint Committee appoints 15 members of a tribunal, five of which are nationals of a member State of the EU, five are Canadians, and five are nationals of third countries.[86] To be selected, tribunal members need to possess the qualifications required in their respective countries for appointment to judicial office, or be jurists of recognized competence and demonstrated expertise in public international law. It is desirable that they have expertise in international investment law, in international trade law and the resolution of disputes arising thereunder.[87] The Joint Committee can also decide to increase or to decrease the number of the members, always by multiples of three.[88] Members are be appointed for a five-year term, renewable once and vacancies are filled as they arise.[89] A President and Vice-President of the tribunal are also appointed from among the Tribunal's third-country members and serve for a two-year term. They are responsible for organizational issues.[90]

The CETA tribunal of first instance would hear cases in divisions of three members, one of whom would be a national of an EU State, one Canadian, and one a national of a third country.[91] Divisions are always to be chaired by the member who is a national of the third country.[92] Divisions are required to be composed within 90 days of the submission of a claim.[93] The President

83 European Commission proposes signature and conclusion of Japan and Singapore agreements (April 18, 2018) see http://trade.ec.europa.eu/doclib/press/index.cfm?id=1826.
84 Commission presents EU-Vietnam trade and investment agreements for signature and conclusion (Oct. 17, 2018) http://trade.ec.europa.eu/doclib/press/index.cfm?id=1921.
85 *See* http://ec.europa.eu/trade/policy/in-focus/eu-mexico-trade-agreement/.
86 CETA Art. 8.27 (2).
87 CETA Art. 8.27 (4).
88 CETA Art. 8.27 (3).
89 CETA Art. 8.27 (5). Note that a person appointed to replace a Member of the Tribunal whose term of office has not expired shall hold office for the remainder of the predecessor's term.
90 CETA Art. 8.27 (8).
91 CETA Art. 8.27 (6).
92 CETA Art. 8.27 (6).
93 CETA Art. 8.27 (7).

of the Tribunal appoints the Members of the Tribunal that compose the division hearing the case on a rotation basis, ensuring that the composition of the divisions is random and unpredictable, while giving equal opportunity to all Members of the Tribunal to serve.[94] Members of the Tribunal are to be paid a monthly retainer fee.

If the Joint Committee fails to make these appointments within 90 days from the date that a claim is submitted for dispute settlement, either disputing party may request the Secretary General of ICSID to appoint a division consisting of three Members of the Tribunal, unless the disputing parties have agreed that the case is to be heard by a sole Member of the Tribunal.[95] The Secretary General of ICSID makes the appointment by random selection from the existing nominations.[96] The Secretary-General of ICSID cannot appoint as chair a national of either Canada or a EU Member State unless the disputing parties agree otherwise.

Disputing parties may agree that a case be heard by a sole Tribunal member selected from the third-country nationals.[97] The respondent is to give "sympathetic consideration" to a request from the claimant to have the case heard by a sole member of the Tribunal, in particular when the claimant is a small or medium-sized enterprise or the compensation or damages claimed are relatively low.[98]

Article 8(28) CETA also establishes an Appellate Tribunal (AT) to review awards rendered by the Tribunal based on errors in the application or interpretation of applicable law, manifest errors in the appreciation of facts, including relevant domestic law, and the grounds for annulment set out in Article 52 of the ICSID Convention.[99] The CETA Joint Committee is to appoint the members of the AT similarly to the way in which it appoints the members of the Tribunal.

The EU-Singapore FTA also envisages a similar approach: it institutes a tribunal of first instance and a Permanent Appeal Tribunal, each composed of six members appointed for terms of eight years—two by the EU, two by Singapore and two jointly—to be paid a retainer fee and a fee for each day worked as a Tribunal Member. Both would hear cases in three-member divisions. The ICSID Secretariat acts as Secretary of the Tribunal.[100] The EU-Vietnam FTA

94 CETA Art. 8.27 (7).
95 CETA Art. 8.27 (17).
96 CETA Art. 8.27 (17).
97 CETA Art. 8.27 (9).
98 CETA Art. 8.27 (9).
99 CETA Art. 8(28).
100 Art. 3.

also includes similar provisions for a permanent bilateral investment court system.[101]

Importantly, CETA also expressly envisages the eventual harmonization of these bilateral investment courts under the separate FTAs into a multilateral Investment Court System (ICS).[102]

It is early to assess how this innovative system will work in practice, or whether or not it could eventually replace ad hoc investment treaty arbitration (which remains the default choice in major recent treaties, such as the Comprehensive and Progressive Agreement for Trans-Pacific Partnership). However, it is clear that the EU proposal for a permanent court has generated a great amount of discussion and scrutiny.[103] It is also proving essential as a tool to stimulate a much-needed discussion about reform of ISDS. As of April 2019, the discussion is still very much on going. Some actors see ISDS as a system that only requires specific and targeted adjustments. Other actors believe that more structural changes are needed, which may include, for example, the creation of an appeal mechanism or a permanent multilateral investment court, as proposed by the EU and Canada.[104] UNICTRAL Working Group III has so far decided to pursue both tracks and has requested the Secretariat to undertake preparatory work on, inter alia, the drafting of a code of conduct for arbitrators, and the selection and appointment of adjudicators, while at the same time preparing a more detailed workplan that could include other potential reform solutions.[105]

---

101 Arts. 12–13.

102 Art. 8.29 (providing that the "The Parties shall pursue with other trading partners the establishment of a multilateral investment tribunal and appellate mechanism for the resolution of investment disputes. Upon establishment of such a multilateral mechanism, the CETA Joint Committee shall adopt a decision providing that investment disputes under this Section will be decided pursuant to the multilateral mechanism and make appropriate transitional arrangements.")

103 On criticisms to ISDS, see in general MICHAEL WAIBEL, ASHA KAUSHAL, KYO-HWA CHUNG AND CLAIRE BALCHIN (eds.), THE BACKLASH AGAINST INVESTMENT ARBITRATION: PERCEPTIONS AND REALITY (2012).

104 For discussion on alternative choices, *see* Sergio Puig, & Gregory Shaffer, *Imperfect Alternatives: Institutional Choice and the Reform of Investment Law*, 112 361 (2018) and Anthea Roberts, *Incremental, Systemic, and Paradigmatic Reform of Investor-State Arbitration*, 112 AM. J. INT'L L. 410.

105 UNCITRAL Working Group III (Investor-State Dispute Settlement Reform), A/CN.9/970—Report of Working Group III (Investor-State Dispute Settlement Reform) on the work of its thirty-seventh session (*advance copy*), 37th Session 1–5 April 2019, available here: https://uncitral.un.org/en/working_groups/3/investor-state.

3.4 *Emergency Arbitrators*

The emergency arbitrator procedure has recently emerged in response to one perceived weakness of international arbitration, namely the difficulty of obtaining urgent relief before the tribunal is constituted. The procedure addresses the need to have an arbitrator capable of issuing preliminary measures prior to the constitution of the tribunal, in recognition of the reality of the length of time necessary for the parties to finalize their choice of arbitrators.

Though this issue is particularly salient in commercial arbitration, it may arise in the context of investment arbitration also. Several arbitral institutions have recently added to their rules specific provisions for the selection of emergency arbitrators, who are generally appointed by the Secretariat or the Board of the institution. Article 29 of the ICC Rules, for example, provides that when a party needs urgent interim or conservatory measures that cannot await the constitution of an arbitral tribunal, it may make an application for such measures to the Secretariat prior to the transmission of the file to the arbitral tribunal. The President of the Court will then appoint an emergency arbitrator within two days.[106] The SCC and LCIA have similar rules, and the appointment of the emergency arbitrator is made by the Board and the Court respectively.[107]

Probably because the need for emergency arbitrators is more often found in commercial arbitration, only the institutions that predominantly assist the parties in commercial arbitrations have so far amended their rules to include emergency arbitrators; ICSID, UNCITRAL or the PCA Rules do not at this stage include provisions for emergency arbitrators. The new ICSID proposal for amendment does not suggest the inclusion of an emergency arbitrator, relying instead on the fact that new treaties offer alternatives to emergency arbitrators by allowing request for provisional measures before domestic courts.[108]

4 The Selection Criteria: Who Should the Parties Select?

Having detailed how the selection process works in the most-often used institutional rules, this section now examines who should be nominated, and thus be asked to decide the case, and the qualities that arbitrators must and should possess.

106 ICC Rules, Art. 29 and Appendix V, Art. 2.

107 SCC Appendix II, LCIA Art. 9.B.

108 ICSID Secretariat, Proposal for Amendments of ICSID Rules—Working Paper, Volume 3, August 2, 2018, para 492: https://icsid.worldbank.org/en/Documents/Amendments_Vol_3_Complete_WP+Schedules.pdf.

Parties and their counsel spend substantial time and resources selecting the party-appointed arbitrator, which underlines the importance of appointments.[109] Proposed arbitrators' backgrounds are reviewed extensively, including for their nationality, education, professional experience, and technical expertise. Importantly, their arbitration experience is scrutinized, including prior decisions and academic writings, and any previous professional positions and relations, including their prior interactions and relationships with counsel and co-arbitrators in the case.[110] In selecting their candidates, parties also take into consideration the applicable law, the forum, the kind of dispute, the location, the nationality of the parties, and many other issues as well.[111]

The selection is also affected by a party's position in the case. For the claimant, the choice of arbitrator comes early; as the claimant has the right to nominate an arbitrator in the request for arbitration by which the arbitration is commenced. The claimant also has the advantage to go first, and so can spend more time selecting the most suitable arbitrator for the case. Still, the selection of the claimant's arbitrator is also particularly delicate because it is done without knowledge of any of the other members of the tribunal, or counsel for opposing party.[112] The selection is normally done after serious research by counsel representing the claimant in consultation with the client.[113]

The selection of arbitrators by the respondent state is also often complex; as it may involve the advice of several governmental agencies that can potentially be involved in the arbitration, particularly where the case is handled in-house

109 *See* Claudia T. Salomon, *Selecting an International Arbitrator: Five Factors to Consider*, 17 Mealey's Int'l Arb. Rep. 25 (Oct. 2002); *see also* Andreas Lowenfeld, *The Party-Appointed Arbitrator in International Controversies: Some Reflections*, 30 Texas Int'l L. J. 59 (1995); James Wangelin, *Effective Selection of Arbitrators in International Arbitration*, 14 Mealey's Int'l Arb. Rep. 69 (Nov. 1999); R. Doak Bishop & Lucy Reed, *Practical Guidelines for Interviewing, Selecting and Challenging Party-Appointed Arbitrators in International Commercial Arbitration*, 14 Arb. Int'l 395 (1998).

110 Lucy Reed, Jan Paulsson & Nigel Blackaby, Guide to icsid Arbitration 77–79 (2010).

111 *See generally* R. Doak Bishop and Lucy Reed, *Practical Guidelines for Interviewing, Selecting and Challenging Party-Appointed Arbitrators in International Commercial Arbitration*, 14 Arb. Int'l 395 (1998).

112 Waibel & Wu, *supra* note 14, at 13; *see also* C. Giorgetti, *Who Decides Who Decides?*, *supra* note 1.

113 *See, e.g.*, Latham & Watkins, Guide to International Arbitration 8 (2013) (noting that "Parties usually seek advice from their lawyers as to suitable arbitrators. When we advise in this regard, we draw upon our experience of persons with the required attributes (including experience as an arbitrator) and work with our client to identify those arbitrators who we would expect to follow thought processes most in tune with our client's case.").

by government lawyers rather than by external counsel from law firms or barristers' chambers.[114] In the United States, for example, the office of the legal adviser of State Department typically takes the lead, often in consultation with U.S. government offices, including the Departments of Commerce and Treasury and the Office of the U.S. Trade Representative. Given the growing public relevance of international investment arbitration, the selection of the arbitrator by the state also becomes an important instrument for the state to broaden the dispute beyond its bilateral terms and consider the public interests involved.[115] Additionally, the respondent is generally more pressed for time, because they must make a selection within a more limited timeframe.

Applicable rules specify the mandatory characteristics each arbitrator must possess. In the Appendix, Table 3 summarizes the requirements for arbitrators in different rules, including provisions on nationality. Additionally, parties need to consider desirable qualities and other factors, such as legal and professional experience, management experience and time availability.[116]

4.1 *Necessary Requirements*

The applicable rules of procedure mandate that arbitrators must possess certain threshold qualities. Often, these are limited to nationality requirements and the overall essential quality of independence and impartiality.

4.1.1 Nationality

Nationality is an important identifier and under most rules there is a strong preference not to choose an arbitrator of the nationality of the parties.[117] Indeed, the reasons for the exclusion of arbitrators who are nationals of one of the parties can be found in the presumption that an arbitrator who is a national of one of the parties may be too inclined and sympathetic towards the position of a party with which it shares a nationality bond.[118]

---

114 *See generally* Jeremy Sharpe, *Representing Respondent*, in LITIGATING INTERNATIONAL INVESTMENT DISPUTES, C. GIORGETTI (ed.), supra note 1.

115 *See, e.g.*, George H. Aldrich, *The Selection of Arbitrators, in* THE IRAN-UNITED STATES CLAIMS TRIBUNAL AND THE PROCESS OF INTERNATIONAL CLAIMS RESOLUTION (David Caron and John Crook eds., Brill, 2000) (discussing in some detail the process for choosing the third-country arbitrators at the Iran-US Claims Tribunal).

116 *See* Salomon, *supra* note 109.

117 Leigh Swigart, *National Judge: Some Reflections on Diversity in International Courts and Tribunals*, 42 MCGEORGE L. REV. 224 (2010) (observing that "as an identifier, nationality suggests more than a mere category of citizenship or allegiance to a particular state").

118 As Redfern and Hunter acutely note, "the fact that an arbitrator is of a neutral nationality is no guarantee of independence and impartiality. However, the appearance is better and thus it is a practice that is generally followed." ALAN REDFERN, MARTIN HUNTER, NIGEL

Under both ICISD and UNCITRAL rules, certain nationality restrictions apply. Under Article 39 of the ICSID Convention, the majority of the tribunal must be composed of nationals of states other than of the contracting state party to the dispute and the contracting state whose national is a party to the dispute.[119] Rule 1(3) of the ICSID Arbitration Rules requires the consent of the other party to appoint an arbitrator who has the same nationality of the appointing party.[120]

The UNCITRAL Rules also contain similar nationality restrictions, but are somewhat less stringent in relation to nationality requirements. Article 7 requires only that the appointing authority take into account "the advisability of appointing an arbitrator of a nationality other than the nationalities of the parties."[121]

The SCC Rules are more limited.[122] They require the Chairperson of the arbitral tribunal to be of a different nationality than that of the parties, unless otherwise agreed by the parties or deemed appropriate by the Board of Directors of the SCC Institute.[123]

The LCIA Rules are more specific. Article 6 provides that if the parties are of different nationalities, a sole arbitrator or the presiding arbitrator cannot have the same nationality, unless otherwise agreed in writing by all parties.[124] Interestingly, Article 6.2 specifies that the nationality of a party also includes the nationality of the controlling shareholders or interests.[125] This takes into consideration recent criticism to the appointment system as well as the realities

---

BLACKABY & CONSTANTINE PARTASIDES, REDFERN AND HUNTER ON ARBITRATION 263 (Oxford University Press, 2009).

119 ICSID Rules, *supra* note 18, Art. 39 (stating "The majority of the arbitrators shall be national of States other than the Contracting State party to the dispute and the Contracting State whose national is a part to the dispute and the Contracting State whose national is a party to the dispute; provided, however, that the foregoing provisions of this Article shall not apply if the sole arbitrator or each individual member of the Tribunal has been appointed by agreement of the parties.").

120 ICSID Rules of Procedure for Arbitration Rule 3 (stating "(1) If the Tribunal is to be constituted in accordance with Article 37(2)(b) of the Convention: (a) either party shall in a communication to the other party: (i) name two persons, identifying one of them, who shall not have the same nationality as nor be a national of either party, as the arbitrator appointed by it, and the other as the arbitrator proposed to be the President of the Tribunal.").

121 UNCITRAL Rules (1976), Art. 6(4); UNCITRAL Rules (2010), Art. 6(7).

122 SCC Rules (2007), Art. 15(5), *available at* http://cn.cietac.org/Hezuo/4_5.pdf.

123 Note that the role of the Board, similarly to the ICC Court, is limited to the administration of the dispute under the SCC Rules. SCC Rules, Art. 6, Appx. I; *see also id.* Arts. 1–5 and 7.

124 LCIA Art. 6.

125 LCIA Art. 6.1.

of international business, which often includes complex relations. Further, Article 6.3 specifies that "a person who is a citizen of two or more states shall be treated as a national of each state; citizens of the European Union shall be treated as nationals of its different member states and shall not be treated as having the same nationality; a citizen of a state's overseas territory shall be treated as a national of that territory and not of that state; and a legal person incorporated in a state's overseas territory shall be treated as such and not (by such fact alone) as a national of or a legal person incorporated in that State."[126]

The ICC Rules provide, at Article 13(5), that while a sole arbitrator and the presiding arbitrator should not be nationals of any of the parties, in suitable circumstances and if the parties do not object, they could be chosen from a country of nationality of one of the parties.[127]

Of note, however, nationality requirements may be different under a specific investment treaty. Under Article 1125 of NAFTA, for example, parties may agree to appoint arbitrators regardless of their nationality.[128] And indeed, under these rules it is customary for parties to appoint arbitrators of their own nationality.

4.1.2 Impartiality and Independence

All arbitration rules require arbitrators to be impartial and independent. Impartiality fundamentally means that an arbitrator is not partial—or biased—in favor or against one of the parties in the case. An independent arbitrator is one who does not depend—financially, professionally, personally or in any other way—on either of the parties.[129]

Both qualities are necessary for arbitrators to perform their adjudicative functions. These requirements represent the very essence of international investment arbitration, and are expressed in a different, yet similar, way in

---

126 LCIA Art. 6.3.

127 ICC Rules, Art. 13(5).

128 NAFTA, Art. 1125 (providing, in part, that "For purposes of Article 39 of the ICSID Convention and Article 7 of Schedule C to the ICSID Additional Facility Rules, and without prejudice to an objection to an arbitrator based on Article 1124(3) or on a ground other than nationality: (a) the disputing Party agrees to the appointment of each individual member of a Tribunal established under the ICSID Convention or the ICSID Additional Facility Rules ...").

129 For an overview of the discussion, including possible solutions, see Chiara Giorgetti, *Independence and Impartiality of Arbitrators in Investor-State Arbitration: Perceived Problems and Possible Solutions*, EJIL Talk, Apr. 4, 2019, available at: https://www.ejiltalk.org/independence-and-impartiality-of-arbitrators-in-investor-state-arbitration-perceived-problems-and-possible-solutions/.

applicable arbitration rules.[130] Under the ICSID Rules, arbitrators need to "be relied upon to exercise independent judgment."[131] The UNCITRAL Rules require arbitrators to be "independent and impartial."[132] Under the SCC Rules, every arbitrator must be impartial and independent.[133] The ICC rules provide that "every arbitrator must be and remain impartial and independent of the parties involved in the arbitration."[134]

Upon constitution of the tribunal, each arbitrator is also required to sign a declaration confirming that, to the best of her knowledge, there are no reasons why she should not serve as an arbitrator, that she will keep confidential all information received and that she will "judge fairly as between the parties, according to the applicable law, and shall not accept any instruction or compensation with regard to the proceedings from any source except as provided" by the ICSID Convention.[135]

Under the UNCITRAL Arbitration Rules, as amended in 2013:

---

130 For an excellent and exhaustive analysis of the issue under ICSID and other rules, *see* MARIA NICOLE CLEIS, THE INDEPENDENCE AND IMPARTIALITY OF ICSID ARBITRATORS—CURRENT CASE LAW, ALTERNATIVE APPROACHES AND IMPROVEMENT SUGGESTIONS, Brill 2017. See also generally L. Malintoppi, *Arbitrator's Independence and Impartiality*, *in* The Oxford Handbook of International Investment Law 808 (P. Muchlinski et al. eds., 2008).

131 ICSID Rules, *supra* note 18, Art. 14.

132 UNCITRAL Rules (2010), Art. 10(7) & 12(1).

133 SCC Rules, Art. 14.

134 2012 ICC Rules, Art. 11(1).

135 ICSID Arbitration Rules, *supra* note 18, r. 6. The full text of the signed statements states: "To the best of my knowledge there is no reason why I should not serve on the Arbitral Tribunal constituted by the International Centre for Settlement of Investment Disputes with respect to a dispute between ____ and ____. I shall keep confidential all information coming to my knowledge as a result of my participation in this proceeding, as well as the contents of any award made by the Tribunal. I shall judge fairly as between the parties, according to the applicable law, and shall not accept any instruction or compensation with regard to the proceeding from any source except as provided in the Convention on the Settlement of Investment Disputes between States and Nationals of Other States and in the Regulations and Rules made pursuant thereto. Attached is a statement of (a) my past and present professional, business and other relationships (if any) with the parties and (b) any other circumstance that might cause my reliability for independent judgment to be questioned by a party. I acknowledge that by signing this declaration, I assume a continuing obligation promptly to notify the Secretary-General of the Centre of any such relationship or circumstance that subsequently arises during this proceeding." Note that each Arbitrator must sign the declaration before or at the first session of the Tribunal, failing to do so by the end of the first session of the Tribunal shall be deemed tantamount to resignation.

> When a person is approached in connection with his or her possible appointment as an arbitrator, he or she shall disclose any circumstances likely to give rise to justifiable doubts as to his or her impartiality or independence. An arbitrator, from the time of his or her appointment and throughout the arbitral proceedings, shall without delay disclose any such circumstances to the parties and the other arbitrators unless they have already been informed by him or her of these circumstances.[136]

Independence and impartiality are two "distinct but interrelated qualifications, required of every arbitrator" regardless of who appoints them.[137] Under the UNCITRAL Rules the appointing authority is tasked to have regard for considerations that are "are likely to secure the appointment of an independent and impartial arbitrator.[138]

Indeed, the requirement that arbitrators be independent and impartial is probably the most important aspect of an arbitrator's selection. Not only it is the foundation of the specific arbitral proceedings for which the arbitrator is chosen, but it is also at the heart of international arbitration.[139] As

---

136 UNCITRAL Arbitration Rules, art. 11 (as adopted in 2013), available here: https://www.uncitral.org/pdf/english/texts/arbitration/arb-rules-2013/UNCITRAL-Arbitration-Rules-2013-e.pdf. The wording of UNCITRAL Arbitration Rules, art. 11 (2010) are the same, while UNCTRAL Arbitration Rules (1976) read: "A prospective arbitrator shall disclose to those who approach him in connection with his possible appointment any circumstances likely to give rise to justifiable doubts as to his impartiality or independence. An arbitrator, once appointed or chosen, shall disclose such circumstances to the parties unless they have already been informed by him of these circumstances."

137 Noah Rubins & Bernhard Lauterburg, *Independence, Impartiality and Duty of Disclosure in Investment Arbitration, in* INVESTMENT AND COMMERCIAL ARBITRATION—SIMILARITIES AND DIVERGENCES 154 (Christina Knahr, Christian Koller, Walter Rechberger & August Reinisch eds., Eleven International Publishing, 2009). As observed recently by a tribunal rejecting an arbitrator challenge based on alleged lack on impartiality, "the concept of independence and impartiality, though related, are often seen as distinct, although the precise nature of the distinction is not easy to grasp. Generally speaking, independence relates to the lack of relations with a party that may influence an arbitrator's decision. Impartiality, on the other hand, concerns the absence of a bias or predisposition toward one of the parties." *See* Sociedad General de Aguas de Barcelona S.A., and InterAguas Servicios Integrales del Agua S.A. v. The Argentine Republic, ICSID Case No. ARB/03/17, Decision to disqualify on arbitrator, ¶ 30–31 (Oct. 22, 2007) (citations omitted).

138 UNCITRAL Rules (2010), Art. 6(7); UNCITRAL Rules (1976), Art. 6(4).

139 *See* GARY B. BORN, INTERNATIONAL ARBITRATION: LAW AND PRACTICE 130 (Wolters Kluwer, 2012) (observing that independence and impartiality "are fundamental to the arbitral process, which is an adjudicatory procedure requiring a neutral and objective tribunal.").

Professor Andreas Lowenfeld explains, "one of the principal functions of a party-appointed arbitrator is to give confidence in the process to the parties and their counsel."[140] That confidence relies on the appointment by parties of independent and impartial arbitrators that both parties can trust.[141]

Because arbitrators must be trusted by both parties, parties must avoid appointing somebody who could justifiably be considered partial towards their case in the expectation that it will make the case an easier win. An arbitrator who is perceived as partisan will quickly lose influence with the other members of the arbitral tribunal, and especially with the president or chairperson.[142] Additionally, a partisan arbitrator is subject to challenge procedures, which can result in substantial additional costs, protracted arbitral procedures, more acrimonious proceedings, and of course the possible removal of the arbitrator.

Instead, party-appointed arbitrators are nominated with the expectation that they understand the party's position and support their case. It is a delicate line, and one that should never be crossed into partiality. An experienced counsel generally advises on the most appropriate arbitrator for a specific case.[143]

140 *See* Lowenfeld, *supra* note 9, at 62 ("Sometimes that confidence can be based on mutual acquaintances, without direct personal contact; some potential arbitrators become well-known through published writings, lectures, committee work, or public office. Others are not so well known, and I understand that lawyers or clients or both want to have a firsthand look. I think; however, some restraint should be shown by both sides."); *see also* Thomas Franck, *Legitimacy in the International System*, 82 AM. J. INT'L L. 705 (arguing that decision makers who are perceived as legitimate enhance the legitimacy of the dispute resolution system itself).

141 *See* William W. Park, *Arbitrator Integrity, in* THE BACKLASH AGAINST INVESTMENT ARBITRATION 189, 191 (Michael Waibel et al. eds., Wolters Kluwer, 2010) (stating "in a cross-border context, the prohibition on bias justifies itself by reference to the very same goal underlying the decision to arbitrate: promoting a level playing field.").

142 *See* Hans Smit, *The Pernicious Institution of the Party-Appointed Arbitrators*, COLUMBIA FDI PERSPECTIVES, no. 33, Dec. 14, 2010, at 2, *available at* http://www.vcc.columbia.edu/files/vale/print/Perspective_33_Smit_2.pdf (noting that "The presence of a partisan arbitrator on a panel will normally reduce, if not eliminate, the free exchange of ideas among the members of the panel. The chair will be less receptive to arguments that appear to be moved by partisan considerations or may join one of the arbitrators, with the result that the other party-appointed arbitrators feel excluded from the deliberations.").

143 *See* Constantine Partasides, *The Art of Selecting the Right Arbitrator* (lecture, New Academic Building, London School of Economics, London, Eng., Nov. 9, 2011), *available at* http://www.lse.ac.uk/newsAndMedia/videoAndAudio/channels/publicLecturesAndEvents/player.aspx?id=1252 (arguing that the most important issue to properly select an arbitrator is to have a legal theory that supports the case and then to walk backwards to find the most appropriate arbitrator that would likely support that legal theory).

It is incumbent upon the arbitrators to disclose any fact that could be reasonably considered as possible grounds for disqualification.[144] The UNCITRAL Rules provide that "when a person is approached in connection with his or her possible appointment as an arbitrator, he or she shall disclose any circumstances likely to give rise to justifiable doubts as to his or her impartiality or independence."[145] Similarly, ICSID Arbitration Rule 6 requires arbitrators to disclose all "past and present professional, business and other relationships (if any) with the parties and any other circumstances that might cause my reliability for independent judgment to be questioned by the parties." Arbitrators have a continuing duty to provide such information to the Secretary General and the parties.[146] The ICC Rules require a prospective arbitrator before appointment to disclose to the Secretariat "any facts or circumstances which might be of such a nature as to call into question the arbitrator's independence in the eyes of the parties, as well as any circumstances that could give rise to reasonable doubts as to the arbitrator's impartiality."[147] Under the SCC Rules, "before being appointed as arbitrator, a person shall disclose any circumstances which may give rise to justifiable doubts as to his/her impartiality or independence."[148]

Information that should be disclosed includes any past or present relations with the parties, any financial interests possibly related to the dispute, and any conflict related to the law firm or barristers' chambers of which the arbitrator is a member. It has become more common to use the Guidelines adopted by the International Bar Association on Conflicts of Interests in International Arbitration (IBA Guidelines) to assess the existence of possible conflicts and the extent of any duty of disclosure.[149] The IBA Guidelines offer specific lists of situations that would lead to conflict ("red" list), that exclude conflict ("green" list) and those which may, depending on the specific facts, give rise

144 *See* Rubins & Lauterburg, *supra* note 137, at 153–80.

145 UNCITRAL Rules (2010), Art. 11; *see also* UNCITRAL Rules (1976), Art. 9 (requiring a prospective arbitrator to "disclose to those who approach him in connection with his possible appointment any circumstances likely to give rise to justifiable doubts as to his impartiality or independence. An arbitrator, once appointed or chosen, shall disclose such circumstances to the parties unless they have already been informed by him of these circumstances.").

146 ICSID Arbitration Rules, Rule 6.

147 ICC Rules, Art. 11.

148 SCC Rules, Art. 14(2).

149 Council of the International Bar Association, "IBA Guidelines on Conflict of Interest in International Arbitration" (approved May 22, 2004) [hereinafter "IBA Guidelines"], *available at* http://www.ibanet.org/Publications/publications_IBA_guides_and_free_materials.aspx. In general, see Born, *supra* note 139, at 132–35.

to justifiable doubts as to the independence and impartiality of the arbitrator and that require a duty to disclose ("orange" list).

However, it is notable that there is no code of conduct for arbitrators which clearly defines the duties of impartiality and independence and which sets rules on conflict of interest. Indeed, the issue of codifying applicable ethical rules seem ripe for elaboration, possibly by UNCITRAL Working Group III, which in April 2019 requested the UNCITRAL secretariat to study the issue, together with ICSID.[150]

4.1.3 Legal Expertise and Other Mandated Requirements

Article 14(1) of the ICSID Convention requires that prospective arbitrators be "persons of high moral character and recognized competence in the fields of law, commerce, industry or finance, who may be relied upon to exercise independent judgment."[151] The requirement of high moral character is not further explained, but a similar concept is found in the statutes of most international courts and tribunals.[152]

During the negotiation of the ICSID Convention, states discussed whether arbitrators should be required to be lawyers, but due to the potentially diverse and technical nature of disputes likely to be the subject of ICSID proceedings, it was deemed necessary to allow parties to nominate arbitrators from other fields of expertise as well.[153] Similarly, a proposal that "the highest courts of justice, schools of law, bar associations and other relevant organizations" were consulted prior to arbitrators' appointment to advise on competence never made it to the final draft of the Convention.[154]

Despite not being a mandatory requirement, parties would make a mistake not to appoint a lawyer as their arbitrator. International investment disputes are complex and require deep understanding and familiarity with substantive

150 UNCITRAL, Working Group III, Investor-State Dispute Settlement Reform, http://www.uncitral.org/uncitral/en/commission/working_groups/3Investor_State.html.

151 ICSID Convention, Art. 14.

152 *See, e.g.*, Statute of the International Court of Justice, Art. 2 ("The Court shall be composed of a body of independent judges, elected regardless of their nationality from among persons of high moral character ..."); Rome Statute of the International Criminal Court, Art. 36.3(a) ("The Court shall be composed of a body of independent judges, elected regardless of their nationality from among persons of high moral character ...").

153 *See* KAREL DAELE, CHALLENGE AND DISQUALIFICATION OF ARBITRATORS IN INTERNATIONAL ARBITRATION, 84 (2012) (noting that the rules reflect a compromise: arbitrators do not have to be lawyers but must be reasonably competent in the field of law).

154 *Id.*

and procedural legal issues. An excellent knowledge of diverse bodies of law is essential for a competent arbitrator.

Requirements for additional qualifications may be found in the specific treaty or contract at issue in the dispute, including in terms of specific expertise required from the arbitrator. These may include requirements for arbitrators to be experts in "public international law, international trade or international investment agreements."[155] More often, however, additional mandatory requirements are absent from applicable rules, so that parties enjoy a lot of freedom when making appointments.

4.2 *Desirable Qualities*

International investment arbitrations tend to be complex and often involve two or more legal systems and languages. When selecting an arbitrator, therefore, a party should keep in mind several additional desirable qualities.

To a great extent, desirable qualities that should be taken into consideration depend on the nature of the dispute. Many successful arbitrators tend to come from elite schools and have often obtained advanced degrees, which allow them to be familiar with a variety of legal systems. It is important to consider the legal background of any prospective arbitrator in relation to the applicable law, the applicable rules of arbitration, the nature of the dispute, and the other members of the tribunal.

It is also important to choose someone that has a proven record in international adjudication, and preferably in international investment arbitration, though the record need not necessarily come from practice as arbitrator.[156] In an effort to diversify who is selected as arbitrators, parties should also consider candidates who acquired relevant experience through other international courts, have a background as counsel and experts, or are academics or researchers who have published in the area.

155 *See, e.g.*, Agreement Between the Government of Canada and the Government of the Republic of China for the Promotion and Reciprocal Protection of Investment Arbitration, Art. 24, Sept. 9, 2012.

156 *See* Obadia, *Remarks at 105th ASIL Annual Meeting, supra* note 26, at 76. (Noting that several issues are considered when making an appointment, including "language of the proceedings, but also of the documents, as it may be different." She also explains that, when making appointments "we also look at availability of the arbitrators … experience of the candidate as an arbitrator, not only in investment arbitration but also in commercial arbitration and other types of arbitration … knowledge of the relevant law, which is often public international law, and the knowledge of international investment law, which has become more and more complex." Finally, "the cohesiveness of the tribunal" is also a factor.)

Parties may also wish to select an arbitrator with a demonstrated ability to participate effectively in complex arbitrations or negotiations. This is particularly important for the presiding arbitrator, who plays an important role in developing consensus and ensuring smooth arbitration proceedings. For these reasons, parties often choose to appoint arbitrators that have already served as arbitrators in international investment arbitration. This practice also allows parties to better scrutinize the record of the arbitrator as more of their views and decisions are known and publicly available. However, choosing an experienced arbitrator must also be balanced with the fact that arbitrators who have served in many arbitrations may be more prone to be challenged, both for possible conflicts or repeat appointments by the same counsel or party.[157] Frequently appointed arbitrators may also be already quite busy, thus making a longer process more likely.[158] The call for more diverse appointments relates to these concerns also. Appointing new and diverse arbitrators would address some of these issues.

Additionally, because international investment arbitrations tend to raise numerous public international law issues, including determining the content of customary international law, the applicable sources of law, treaty interpretation, attribution and state responsibility, it is advisable to appoint an arbitrator who understands and knows public international law, either as a practitioner or an academic, or possibly both.

Knowledge of languages is also important. This includes not only the languages of the proceedings, but also the language in which the evidence—both oral and written—is likely to be submitted.[159] Knowledge of languages needs to include drafting ability and is also an important consideration to assess the cohesiveness of the tribunal and the effectiveness of each arbitrator within the tribunal.

157 See for example *Blue Bank International & Trust (Barbados) Ltd. v. Bolivarian Republic of Venezuela*, ICSID Case No. ARB 12/20, Decision on the Parties' Proposals to Disqualify a Majority of the Tribunal (12 Nov. 2013) at: http://www.italaw.com/cases/1513, in which one of the arbitrator was challenged on the claim that he had too often been appointed by claimants and thus had developed a bias on claimant's favor.

158 In a recently decided challenge, for example, Ecuador challenged claimant's appointed arbitrator on the ground, inter alia, that he had been nominated by claimant's counsel eight times. *Burlington Resources, Inc. v. Republic of Ecuador*, ICSID Case No. ARB/08/5, Decision on the Proposal or Disqualification of Professor Francisco Orrego Vicuña, ¶¶ 75, 78–80 (Dec. 13, 2013), *available at* https://icsid.worldbank.org/ICSID; *see* note 107 in this chapter.

159 Obadia, *supra* note 26, at 76 (noting that several issues are considered when making an appointment).

Other important qualities are availability and good time management skills. As international investment arbitrations tend to be long and time consuming, it is often desirable to request the arbitrator's availability before nomination and request that time is set aside for each arbitral proceeding. This has become the modus operandi of several arbitral institutions, including ICSID, and is mandated by the ICC.[160]

Parties should also assess any candidate's ability to work efficiently with the other members of the arbitral panel and the likelihood that the views of the potential arbitrator will be appropriately heard and carry weight with the other arbitrators during the tribunal's deliberations.[161]

Finally, especially when selecting the presiding arbitrator, parties need to consider the overall composition of the tribunal, in terms of languages, past experience and past common arbitral and professional experience.[162] Members of the arbitral tribunal are likely to work long hours together so it is important to consider languages, training and experience in that context also. Moreover, harmony among the members of the arbitral tribunal is also important because it will more likely result in a cohesive award which is decided unanimously, rather than by majority.[163] It may also reduce the likelihood of dissenting awards, which are often seen as undesirable and may lead to challenges or annulment proceedings.[164]

---

160 ICC Rules, Art. 13(1).

161 Obadia, *supra* note 26, at 76 (noting issues considered when making an appointment include "the cohesiveness of the tribunal.").

162 *See* Redfern, Hunter, Blackaby & Partasides, *supra* note 118, at 263 (observing that the task of presiding over an international arbitration "is no less skilled than that of a surgeon conducting an operation or a pilot flying an aircraft. It should not be entrusted to someone with no practical experience of it.").

163 In its Guide to International Arbitration, Latham & Watkins suggest considering the following issues when selecting an arbitrator: "the candidate's familiarity with the governing law and the applicable arbitration rules; the candidate's background (e.g., legal training and experience, experience in the relevant industry or similar industries); the language and the place of the arbitration; the candidate's writings (although many arbitrators are guarded in their publicly expressed views) and past decisions/awards to the extent known or available; our interactions with the candidate in previous arbitrations or at conferences, the views of our colleagues and the candidate's general reputation; and the candidate's ability to influence the selection of the Chairman/President and the likelihood that the candidate's views will carry weight with the other arbitrators during deliberations." Latham & Watkins, GUIDE TO INTERNATIONAL ARBITRATION 8 (2013).

164 On dissenting opinions, *see generally*, Albert van den Berg, *Dissenting Opinions by Party-Appointed Arbitrators in Investment Arbitration,* in LOOKING TO THE FUTURE: ESSAYS ON INTERNATIONAL LAW IN HONOR OF W. MICHAEL REISMAN 824 (Arsanjani et al. eds., 2010).

These mix of required and desirable qualities result in the selection of a small group of talented international arbitrators, who are generally experienced lawyers of high international standing, often multilingual and capable of handling complex cases involving complicated sets of facts, diverse applicable law and rules of procedures, and multi-cultural parties.[165] Most generally, the group is composed of international law practitioners, including law firm partners and barristers in private practice, former high-ranking government officials and some public international law professors.[166] Critics, however, point out that the system has also resulted in the selection of a small number of repeat players who lack diversity.[167] This is likely the result of the parties trying to selected a "known" arbitrator whose decisions may be seen as somehow predictable based on the arbitrator's awards in previous cases. An important consequence of this practice, however, is the potential increase in conflicts of interest of the appointed arbitrators.[168] These include possible conflicts arising from multiple appointments of the same arbitrator by the same law-firm or the same party, the appointment of the same arbitrators in similar cases (which may give rise to issue-conflict), or the practice of double-hatting, by which a person acts both as counsel and arbitrator in different investment arbitration cases under the same or different rules that may possibly involve similar issues.[169] The call for increased diversity and the proposal for the creation of a permanent court are responsive of these concerns.

---

165 *See* Catherine Rogers, *The Vocation of International Arbitrators*, 20 Am. U. Int'l L. Rev. 958, 958–59 (2005).

166 A recent article by Malcolm Langford, Daniel Behn and Runar Hilleren Lie provides a thorough analysis of who sits in investment arbitrations, see Malcolm Langford, Daniel Behn and Runar Hilleren Lie, *The Revolving Door in International Investment Arbitration,* Journal of International Economic Law, Volume 20, Issue 2 (2017), p. 301 (see especially Table 1).

167 *See, e.g.*, Sergio Puig, *Social Capital in the Arbitration Market*, 25 (2014) 387. *See also* Charles N. Brower; Stephen W. Schill, *Is Arbitration a Threat or a Boom to the Legitimacy of International Investment* Law, 9 Chi. J. Int'l L. 471, 498 (2009).

168 *See* Gabriel Bottini, *Should Arbitrator Live on Mars—Challenge of Arbitrators in Investment Arbitration*, 32 Suffolk Transnat'l L. Rev. 341, 366 (2009). See also Luke A. Sobota, *Repeat Appointments in International Investment Disputes,* in Challenges and Recusals of Judges and Arbitrators in International Courts and Tribunals (Chiara Giorgetti, ed., 2015) (henceforth Giorgetti, Challenges and Recusals).

169 On issue conflict, *see* John Crook and Laurence Boisson de Chazournes, *ASIL-ICCA Task Force Report on Issue Conflicts in Investor-State Arbitration*, available at: https://www.arbitration-icca.org/projects/Issue_Conflict.html. For a nuanced analysis of a specific case on issue conflict, see Romain Zamour, *Issue Conflicts and the Reasonable Expectation of an Open Mind: The Challenge Decision in Devas v. India and Its Impact*, in Giorgetti, Challenges and Recusals, *supra* note 168.

Some counsel will contact potential arbitrators prior to appointment to assess their suitability, availability, and interest in the case. This practice is known as "interviewing" arbitrators and it is not uniformly approved. Some arbitrators find it improper to discuss any issues related to a potential appointment; others do not want to subject themselves to this practice as they find intrusive and demening of the judicial function.[170] Under the IBA Guidelines, an arbitrator is not disqualified if she or he has an initial contact with the appointing party prior to the appointment provided that that contact "is limited to the arbitrator's availability and qualifications to serve or to the names of possible candidates for a chairperson and did not address the merits or procedural aspects of the dispute." While interviews are becoming more common and accepted, counsel must be very conscious of their limitations and must avoid creating a conflict where none existed by discussing any specific procedural or substantive aspects of the case.[171] As general guidance, those present during the interview should behave as if the opposing party was also present in the meeting.[172]

4.3 *The Quest for Diversity*

One well-placed criticism of international investment arbitration is the lack of diversity among arbitrators. Evidence clearly shows that the great majority of arbitrators are white men from Western countries.[173] The multiple advantages of diversity, both in terms of legitimacy of the process and of the result for both parties and stakeholders, leave little doubt as to the necessity of

170 *See* Redfern, Hunter, Blackaby & Partasides, *supra* note 118, at 264 (stating that "a number of European arbitrators have declined to participate in such events [interviews] on the grounds that they were at best demeaning, and at worst improper.").

171 *See* Redfern, Hunter, Blackaby & Partasides, *supra* note 118, at 264–65 (observing that "it is hard to perceive the practice as being objectionable in principle; provided that is not done in a secretive way and that the scope of the discussion is appropriately restricted. In particular, it is quite appropriate for a prospective arbitrator to be questioned in person on matters relating to the existence of conflict interest.[...] [H]e or she may also be questioned on their experience in the relevant field, qualification for the case in hand, as well as availability. It is also reasonable for a party's representatives to have on opportunity to assess the candidate's physical and mental health. However, there should be no probing of the prospective arbitrator's view on the merits of the case.").

172 *See* Born, *supra* note 139, at 126.

173 Malcolm Langford, Daniel Behn, and Runer Hilleren Lie, *The Revolving Door in International Investment Arbitration*, 20 JOURNAL OF INTERNATIONAL ECONOMIC LAW 301, 313 (2017), see also Sergio Puig, *Social Capital in the Arbitration Market*, 25 EUR. J. INT'L L. 387 (2014).

fostering diversity.[174] The problem, in a system based on party-autonomy, is how to encourage this change. Counsel may be hesitant to advise a client to select someone without a track-record, and whose views may be more difficult to ascertain. Detailed review of past decisions is an essential tool used by counsel in the selection of arbitrators, and of course those individuals who have been previously appointed have a more substantial record. That said, the call for increased diversity is strong and the advantages and necessity of diversity are recognized by all players in the system. Thus, to break the vicious circle on repeat appointment, several initiatives have been launched. One such initiative is the "Equal Representation in Arbitration Pledge" which seeks to improve the profile and representation of women in international arbitration as well as to appoint women as arbitrators on an equal opportunity basis. The Pledge is open to both institutions and individuals and has so far been signed by more than 3,500 individuals and institutions.[175] Appointing authorities and institutions have been first movers on this issue and have generally recently tried to appoint a newer and more diverse cadre of arbitrators. For example, the most recent list of Arbitrators and Conciliators Designation by the ICSID Chairperson, which must be used for appointments made by ICSID, includes equal representation of female and male candidates as well as significant geographical diversity. In the on-going discussion about reforming international investment arbitration, implementing diversity is certainly topical. It also moves the needle in support of more numerous appointments by third-parties, be those appointing authorities, institutions or in permanent courts.[176]

5 Constitution of the Tribunal

Once the arbitrators are selected, the institution that administers the proceedings steps in and requires the arbitrator to fulfill certain administrative and disclosure acts. These confirm the appointments and result in the constitution of the tribunal and, in most cases, the formal commencement of the arbitral

174 *See, e.g.*, Nienke Grossman, *The Normative Legitimacy of International Courts*, 86 Temple L. Rev. 61 (2013), *Shattering the Glass Ceiling in International Adjudication*, 56 Va. J. Int'l L. 339 (2016) and *Achieving Sex Representative International Court Benches*, 110 Am. J. Int'l L. 82 (2016).

175 *See* Equal Representation in Arbitration, About the Pledge, available at: http://www.arbitrationpledge.com.

176 For an exhaustive discussion, including possible solutions, *see* Andrea K. Bjorklund, *The Diversity Deficit in Investment Arbitration*, EJILTalk! April 4, 2019, available at: https://www.ejiltalk.org/the-diversity-deficit-in-investment-arbitration/.

proceedings. The specific procedures required for the final constitution of the tribunal vary.

Under ICSID, the Secretary General must be notified of the appointments. As soon as the Secretary-General is informed by a party or the Chairman of the Administrative Council of the appointment of an arbitrator, the Secretary General will seek the appointee's acceptance.[177] The arbitrator must confirm the appointment within fifteen days, failure of which will result in the appointment of a new arbitrator. The tribunal is deemed constituted and the proceedings begin on the date on which the Secretary General notifies the parties that all arbitrators have accepted the appointment.[178] Before or at the first session of the tribunal, each arbitrator is required to sign a declaration of independence and confidentiality.[179] Any arbitrator that fails to sign the declaration by the end of the first session of the tribunal is deemed to have resigned from the arbitral tribunal.[180]

Similarly, the ICC rules require a prospective arbitrator to sign a statement of "acceptance, availability, impartiality and independence" before appointment or confirmation. The prospective arbitrator must also disclose in writing to the Secretariat any facts or circumstances that may call into question the arbitrator's independence in the eyes of the parties, as well as any circumstances that could give rise to any reasonable doubts as to his or her impartiality. The Secretariat will then provide the information to the parties in writing and fix a time limit for any comments from them.[181]

177 ICSID Rules, *supra* note 18, Rule 5.

178 ICSID Rules, *supra* note 18, Rule 6.

179 The declaration states: "To the best of my knowledge there is no reason why I should not serve on the Arbitral Tribunal constituted by the International Centre for Settlement of Investment Disputes with respect to a dispute between (party) and (party). I shall keep confidential all information coming to my knowledge as a result of my participation in this proceeding, as well as the contents of any award made by the Tribunal. I shall judge fairly as between the parties, according to the applicable law, and shall not accept any instruction or compensation with regard to the proceeding from any source except as provided in the Convention on the Settlement of Investment Disputes between States and Nationals of Other States and in the Regulations and Rules made pursuant thereto. Attached is a statement of (a) my past and present professional, business and other relationships (if any) with the parties and (b) any other circumstance that might cause my reliability for independent judgment to be questioned by a party. I acknowledge that by signing this declaration, I assume a continuing obligation promptly to notify the Secretary-General of the Centre of any such relationship or circumstance that subsequently arises during this proceeding." *Id.*

180 *Id.*

181 ICSID Rules, *supra* note 18, Art. 11.

The procedure under the ICC Rules also includes an additional confirmation of the arbitrators' nomination by the Secretary General and the Court. The Secretary General confirms the nomination provided that the statement they have submitted contains no qualification regarding impartiality or independence or if that qualification has not given rise to any objections. The confirmation is reported to the Court at its next session. If the Secretary General considers the prospective arbitrator should not be confirmed, the matter is referred to the Court.[182] In confirming arbitrators, the Court considers the prospective arbitrator's nationality, residence, and other relationships with the countries of which the parties or the other arbitrators are nationals, as well as the prospective arbitrator's availability and ability to conduct the arbitration in accordance with the Rules.[183] The decisions of the Court as to the appointment, confirmation, challenge or replacement of an arbitrator are final, and their reasons remain confidential.[184] As soon as the tribunal is constituted, and provided that the advance on costs is paid, the Secretariat transmits the file of the case to the arbitral tribunal.[185]

Under the SCC Rules, the prospective arbitrator must submit to the secretariat a signed statement of impartiality and independence which discloses any circumstances that may give rise to justifiable doubts as to his or her impartiality or independence. The Secretariat provides the parties with a copy of the statement.[186] When the arbitral tribunal is appointed and the advance cost is paid, the Secretariat refers the case to the arbitral tribunal, which begins its work.[187]

The UNCITRAL rules are less detailed and require the arbitrator, from the time of the appointment and throughout the arbitral proceedings, to disclose without delay any such circumstances to the parties and the other arbitrators unless they have already been informed by him or her of these circumstances.[188]

---

182 ICSID Rules, *supra* note 18, Art. 13(2).

183 ICC Rules, Art. 13(1). On the ICC practice concerning confirmation, see Anne Marie Whitesell, *Independence In ICC Arbitration: ICC Court Practice Concerning Appointment, Confirmation, Challenges And Replacement of Arbitrators, in* THE INDEPENDENCE OF ARBITRATORS ICC, INTERNATIONAL COURT OF ARBITRATION BULLETIN 7 (Spec. Supp., 2008).

184 ICC Rules, Art. 11(4).

185 ICC Rules, Art. 16.

186 SCC Rules, Art. 14(3).

187 SCC Rules, Art. 18.

188 UNCITRAL Rules (2010), Art. 11; *see also* UNCITRAL Rules (1976), Art. 9 ("A prospective arbitrator shall disclose to those who approach him in connection with his possible appointment any circumstances likely to give rise to justifiable doubts as to his impartiality or independence. An arbitrator, once appointed or chosen, shall disclose such

6 Removal of Arbitrators

The right of a party to challenge an arbitrator's appointment is a fundamental factor that contributes to the perceived legitimacy of each member of the arbitral tribunal. This section explains and compares the main rules applicable to challenges with a specific eye on identifying the different elements that may strengthen and undermine the legitimacy of the members of the tribunal and of the arbitration process generally. Indeed, challenge procedures are one of the most important control mechanisms that ensures the legitimacy of the international investment arbitration process. Challenges provide a remedy to the possible abuse of the arbitration process by a party via its right to appoint an arbitrator.[189]

Grounds for challenging an arbitrator are generally limited to an alleged lack of the qualities needed to be an arbitrator, which as seen above most often revolve around an asserted lack of independence and impartiality. The proper applicable standards may differ, and the applicable rules should be closely examined when considering a challenge.[190]

As with the discussion of the appointment of arbitrators in the previous section, this section likewise examines and explains applicable challenge rules in the most common applicable rules, namely those of the ICSID, UNCITRAL, the PCA, the SCC, the LCIA and the ICC. This section first explores the applicable procedure for challenging an arbitrator. It then analyzes the main reasons for challenges and evaluates some relevant challenges cases.

6.1 *Procedure*

Challenge procedures require a party to rise any issue that may create doubts as to the independence and impartiality of the selected arbitrator within a specified amount of time, which varies depending on the institution and is generally relatively short. This is important because the procedure must respect the rights of both parties: the right of the challenger to rise any doubt

circumstances to the parties unless they have already been informed by him of these circumstances.").

189 *See generally* GIORGETTI, CHALLENGES AND RECUSALS, *supra* note 168, L. Malintoppi and Alvin Yap, *Challenges of Arbitrators in Investment Arbitration,*—Still Work in Progress?, Karel Daele, CHALLENGES AND DISQUALIFICATION ON ARBITRATORS IN INTERNATIONAL ARBITRATION (2012) and James Crawford, *Challenges to Arbitrators in ICSID Arbitration*, in D. Caron et al (eds), PRACTICING VIRTUE: INSIDE INTERNATIONAL ARBITRATION (2015).

190 *See generally* C. Giorgetti, *Challenges of International Investment Arbitrators: How Does it Work And Does it Work?* 2 WORLD ARB. AND MED. REV. (2013).

it has, and the right of the other party not to have the arbitral process delayed or frustrated by vexatious challenges. Once the challenge is filed, there is a procedure to hear the challenge. Both parties are heard, and the challenged arbitrator/s are given the opportunity to respond and address any issue. Often, the underlying arbitral procedure is suspended while the challenge is resolved. An important issue is who decides the challenge. In general, who decides the challenge is linked to who appointed the arbitrator. In most cases, it is therefore the appointing authority that decides on the challenge. As explained below, ICSID is an outlier as challenge to one arbitrator are decided by the remaining arbitrators, while challenges to two or more arbitrators or to the sole arbitrator are decided by the Chair of the Administrative Council of ICSID (the President of the World Bank).

6.1.1 International Convention on the Settlement of Investment Disputes

Challenges procedures under ICSID are quite unique.[191] Article 57 of the ICSID Convention provides that a party may propose the disqualification of an arbitrator "on account of any fact indicating a manifest lack of the qualities" required to be nominated.[192] Though arbitrators' challenges under ICSID are becoming more common, they are still quite rare and they are rarely successful. As of May 2019, only 4 of the 74 disqualification proposals brought under ICSID were upheld.[193]

Challenges proposals under ICSID must be filed with the Secretary General "promptly" and in any case before the proceedings are declared closed.[194] The

191 *See generally* James Crawford, *Challenges to Arbitrators in ICSID Arbitration*, supra note 189.

192 ICSID Rules, *supra* note 18, Art. 57 (stating that "A party may propose to a Commission or Tribunal the disqualification of any of its members on account of any fact indicating a manifest lack of the qualities required by paragraph (1) of Article 14. A party to arbitration proceedings may, in addition, propose the disqualification of an arbitrator on the ground that he was ineligible for appointment to the Tribunal under Section 2 of Chapter IV.").

193 ICSID, Decisions of Disqualification, available at: https://icsid.worldbank.org/en/Pages/Process/Decisions-on-Disqualification.aspx.

194 ICSID Rules, *supra* note 18, Rule 9 (detailing the procedure to be taken: "(1) A party proposing the disqualification of an arbitrator pursuant to Article 57 of the Convention shall promptly, and in any event before the proceeding is declared closed, file its proposal with the Secretary-General, stating its reasons therefor. (2) The Secretary-General shall forthwith: (a) transmit the proposal to the members of the Tribunal and, if it relates to a sole arbitrator or to a majority of the members of the Tribunal, to the Chairman of the Administrative Council; and (b) notify the other party of the proposal. (3) The arbitrator to whom the proposal relates may, without delay, furnish explanations to the Tribunal or the Chairman, as the case may be. (4) Unless the proposal relates to a majority of

Secretary General then transmits the proposal to the members of the tribunal and notifies the other party. If the challenge relates to a sole arbitrator or the majority of the tribunal, the file is also transmitted to the Chairperson of the Administrative Council. The challenged arbitrator is then invited to give explanations to the tribunal or the Chairperson. The remaining members of the tribunal consider and vote on the proposal.[195] Only if the remaining members are equally divided or if the disqualification proposal pertains to the sole arbitrator or to majority of the tribunal, the Chairperson decides on the challenges, using his (or hers) best efforts to make a decision within thirty days after s/he has received the proposal. Pending the decision, the proceedings are suspended.

Under the ICSID's rules, the requirement that an arbitrator's lack of qualities must be "manifest" has traditionally been applied strictly. In *Conoco Philips v. Venezuela*, for example, the tribunal rejected the application to disqualify an arbitrator and recalled that ICSID decisions recognized that the term "manifest" in Article 57 of the Convention meant "obvious" or "evident" and highly probable, and not just possible. Indeed, it imposed a relatively heavy burden on the party proposing disqualification that the manifest lack of the required qualities to sit as an arbitrator had to appear from objective evidence.[196]

---

the members of the Tribunal, the other members shall promptly consider and vote on the proposal in the absence of the arbitrator concerned. If those members are equally divided, they shall, through the Secretary-General, promptly notify the Chairman of the proposal, of any explanation furnished by the arbitrator concerned and of their failure to reach a decision. (5) Whenever the Chairman has to decide on a proposal to disqualify an arbitrator, he shall use his best efforts to take that decision within 30 days after he has received the proposal. (6) The proceeding shall be suspended until a decision has been taken on the proposal.").

195 Note that the recent ICSID decision to disqualify an arbitrator is only the second successful challenge procedure in ICSID proceedings. The challenge was motivated by the fact that, inter alia, that arbitrator had been nominated by claimant's counsel eight times. The challenge on this point was rejected, but it was upheld as the ICSID Chairman considered that the allegations about the ethics of counsel raised by the challenged arbitrators manifestly evidenced an appearance of lack of impartiality. *Burlington Resources, Inc. v. Republic of Ecuador*, ICSID Case No. ARB/08/5, Decision on the Proposal or Disqualification of Professor Francisco Orrego Vicuña, para. 75, 78–80 (Dec. 13, 2013); *see also* Crawford, *supra* note 189.

196 *Id.* para. 56. Similarly, other ICSID Tribunals deciding proposal for the disqualification of members of the arbitral tribunal confirmed that the term manifest meant "obvious" or "evident" and that such a finding would require "obvious evidence" of a state of mind lacking independence or impartiality. For a well reasoned explanation and summary, *see Sociedad General de Aguas de Barcelona S.A. and Vivendi Universal S.A v. Argentina*, ICSID Case No. ARB/03/19, Decision on the Proposal for the Disqualification of a Member of the Arbitral

The strict threshold required to challenge an arbitrator and the fact that decisions are taken by the tribunal's remaining members distinguishes ICSID from other arbitration settings. More recently, ICSID tribunals have somehow seemingly refined the interpretation of "manifest" so as to be closer to other common arbitration rules pertaining to challenges. For example, in *Blue Bank v. Venezuela*, the Chairperson of the ICSID Administrative Council interpreted the manifest standard differently.[197] In that case, Venezuela had challenged the claimant-appointed arbitrator, alleging that the international law firm in which he was a partner also represented a client against Venezuela in another investment arbitration, albeit from a different office. The Chairperson applied "an objective standard based on a reasonable evaluation of the evidence by a third party" and interpreted the word "manifest" in the ICSID Convention "as meaning 'evident' and 'obvious' and relating to the ease with which the alleged lack of qualities can be perceived."[198] Hence, the Chairman interpreted Article 57 of the Convention from the point of view of "reasonable" interpretation from a third party, rather than requiring an stringent objective demonstration of bias as applied by previous tribunals.

It is noteworthy that in the ongoing Rules Amendment Project undertaken by ICSID, there is a proposal to change the rules on challenges so as to better align them with other existing procedures. An amended ICSID Arbitration Rule 30 would allow the two deciding arbitrators hearing a challenge of their co-arbitrator to send the challenge to the Chair of the Administrative Tribunal if they are unable to decide the challenge for any reason, not only if they are divided.[199] This would be a welcomed and overdue change. Given the

---

Tribunal, para. (Oct. 22, 2007), available at https://icsidworldbank.org/ICSID/FrontServlet?requestType=CasesRH&actionVal=showDoc&docId=DC550_En&caseId=C159 (concluding at para. 28 that it "agree[d] with earlier panels which have had to interpret and apply Article 57 that the mere existence of some professional relationship with a party is not an automatic basis for disqualification of an arbitrator or Committee member. All the circumstances need to be considered in order to determine whether the relationship is significant enough to justify entertaining reasonable doubts as to the capacity of the arbitrator or member to render a decision freely and independently.").

197 *Blue Bank Int'l & Trust (Barbados) Ltd. v. Bolivarian Republic of Venezuela*, ICSID Case No. ARB/12/20, Decision on the Parties' Proposals to Disqualify a Majority of the Tribunal, paras. 22–26 (Nov. 12, 2013) (In the case, the respondent had challenged the arbitrator appointed by claimant because of his partnership in the Madrid office of Baker & McKenzie. At the time, Baker & McKenzie also represented claimant in another case against Venezuela through its offices in New York and Caracas).

198 *Id.* at para. 61.

199 *See generally*, ICSID, Amendment Synopsys, https://icsid.worldbank.org/en/amendments/Documents/Homepage/Amendments-Vol_1_Synopsis_EN,FR,SP.pdf and *see also* C. Giorgetti, *Commentary of the Proposed Amendment of the ICSID Arbitration Rules*,

constraints in amending the Convention itself, which requires unanimity of all contracting parties, amending the rules as suggested would also be a realistic goal.

6.1.2 United Nations Commission on International Trade Law

Under the UNCITRAL Rules, a party that intends to challenge an arbitrator must send a notice of the challenge within fifteen days after it has been notified of the appointment of the arbitrator or within fifteen days after learning of the circumstances giving rise to the challenge.[200] The notice of challenge and its reasons are communicated directly to the other party, the arbitrator who is challenged, and to the other arbitrators. If, within fifteen days from the date of the notice, the parties have not agreed on the challenge or the challenged arbitrator has not withdrawn, the party making the challenge may pursue the challenge by seeking, within thirty days from the date of the challenge notice, a decision on the challenge from the appointing authority.[201] A party can challenge the arbitrator it appointed only for reasons the party learnt of after the appointment was made.

Under UNCITRAL Rules, arbitrators may be challenged "if circumstances exist" that give rise to "justifiable doubts" as to the impartiality or independence of an arbitrator.[202] The standard in this case is different from the ICSID "manifest" lack standard and it is generally interpreted as requiring that a reasonable and informed third party would have justifiable doubts as to the

https://icsid.worldbank.org/en/amendments/Documents/Giorgetti_Chiara_Comments_1.26.19.pdf.

200 UNCITRAL Rules (2010), Art. 13 (stating that "A party that intends to challenge an arbitrator shall send notice of its challenge within 15 days after it has been notified of the appointment of the challenged arbitrator, or within 15 days after the circumstances mentioned in articles 11 and 12 became known to that party. 2. The notice of challenge shall be communicated to all other parties, to the arbitrator who is challenged and to the other arbitrators. The notice of challenge shall state the reasons for the challenge. 3. When an arbitrator has been challenged by a party, all parties may agree to the challenge. The arbitrator may also, after the challenge, withdraw from his or her office. In neither case does this imply acceptance of the validity of the grounds for the challenge. 4. If, within 15 days from the date of the notice of challenge, all parties do not agree to the challenge or the challenged arbitrator does not withdraw, the party making the challenge may elect to pursue it. In that case, within 30 days from the date of the notice of challenge, it shall seek a decision on the challenge by the appointing authority.").

201 *Id.*

202 UNCITRAL Rules (2010), Art. 12(1) (stating that "1. Any arbitrator may be challenged if circumstances exist that give rise to justifiable doubts as to the arbitrator's impartiality or independence. 2. A party may challenge the arbitrator appointed by it only for reasons of which it becomes aware after the appointment has been made.").

impartiality of the challenged arbitrator.[203] The combination of the justifiable doubts threshold with the fact that challenge decisions are taken by the appointing authority arguably provides a balanced approach to challenges.[204]

6.1.3 The Stockholm Chamber of Commerce

Under the SCC Rules, a party may challenge an arbitrator if there are circumstances which "give rise to justifiable doubts as to the arbitrator's impartiality or independence" or if the arbitrator does not possess the qualifications agreed by the parties.[205] Any challenge procedure must be submitted in writing to the Secretariat within fifteen days from when the circumstances became known to the party. A failure to challenge within the allotted time constitutes a waiver of the right to make the challenge. The Secretariat notifies the parties and the arbitrators of the challenge and gives them all an opportunity to submit a comment on the challenge. If the other party agrees on the challenge, the arbitrator must resign.[206] In all other cases, the Board of Directors of the SCC Arbitration Institute makes the final decision on the challenge.[207]

6.1.4 The International Chamber of Commerce

The ICC Rules allow a more expansive ground for challenge.[208] The Rules provide that a challenge to an arbitrator, "whether for an alleged lack of impartiality

---

203 *See, e.g., Vito G. Gallo v. Government of Canada*, NAFTA/UNCITRAL, Decision on the Challenge to Mr. J. Christopher Thomas, QC (Oct. 14, 2009), available at http://italaw.com/documents/Gallo-Canada-Thomas_Challenge-Decision.pdf. (holding that that a "reasonable and informed third party" would have had justifiable doubts about Mr. Thomas' impartiality and independence as an arbitrator when also acting as an advisor to NAFTA non-disputing party Mexico).

204 *See, e.g.*, Sarah Grimmer, *The Determination of Arbitrator Challenges by the Secretary-General of the Permanent Court of Arbitration* in GIORGETTI, CHALLENGES AND RECUSALS, *supra* note 168, and infra, section 6.2.

205 SCC Rules, Art. 15.

206 *Id.*

207 *Id.*; *see also* SCC Rules, Art. 16 (Release from Appointment). Note that LCIA Rules also provide that arbitrators can be challenged if circumstances exist that give rise to justifiable doubts as to their independence and impartiality. Challenges must be filed in writing to the LCIA Secretariat within fifteen days from the establishment of the tribunal or from the moment in which the party became aware of the circumstances justifying the challenge. The LCIA Court decides on the challenge in writing. Since 2006, the decisions related to challenges are published in a suitably redacted form. *See* LCIA Rules, Art. 10.

208 ICC Rules, Art. 14 (stating that "1) A challenge of an arbitrator, whether for an alleged lack of impartiality or independence, or otherwise, shall be made by the submission to the Secretariat of a written statement specifying the facts and circumstances on which the challenge is based. 2) For a challenge to be admissible, it must be submitted by a party either within 30 days from receipt by that party of the notification of the appointment or

or independence, or otherwise," must be filed with the Secretariat in writing specifying the facts and circumstances on which the challenge is based. Challenges must be made within thirty days from the appointment or confirmation of the arbitrator, or from the date when the party making the challenge was informed of the relevant facts and circumstances. The Secretariat then offers the opportunity to the arbitrator concerned, the other arbitrators, and the parties to comment in writing. It is for the ICC Court to rule on the admissibility and, at the same time, if necessary, on the merits of a challenge.

6.1.5 The London Court of International Arbitration

The LCIA Court may decide to remove an arbitrator if it has received a written request from the other members of the arbitral tribunal advising that: i) the arbitrator subject to removal has given written notice of his or her intent to resign to the LCIA Court copying all parties and other members of the tribunal; ii) the arbitrator is seriously ill, refuses, or becomes unable or unfit to act; or iii) there are justifiable doubts as to that arbitrator's impartiality or independence.[209] The LCIA Court may decide that the arbitrator is unfit to act when the arbitrator subject to removal i) acts in deliberate violation of the arbitration agreement; ii) does not act fairly or impartially; or iii) does not conduct the arbitration with reasonable efficiency, diligence and industry.[210] If the challenge is to be raised by a party it must do so within 14 days of the formation of the tribunal or (if later) within 14 days of becoming aware of any grounds by submitting a written statement to the LCIA Court, the tribunal, and to other parties.[211] If a party is to challenge an arbitrator whom it participated in appointing or nominated, then it can only do so for reasons of which it becomes aware after the appointment has been made.[212]

Before removal, all parties and challenged arbitrators are provided a reasonable opportunity to comment. The LCIA Court may request further

confirmation of the arbitrator, or within 30 days from the date when the party making the challenge was informed of the facts and circumstances on which the challenge is based if such date is subsequent to the receipt of such notification. 3) The Court shall decide on the admissibility and, at the same time, if necessary, on the merits of a challenge after the Secretariat has afforded an opportunity for the arbitrator concerned, the other party or parties and any other members of the arbitral tribunal to comment in writing within a suitable period of time. Such comments shall be communicated to the parties and to the arbitrators.").

209 LCIA Arbitration Rules Art. 10(1).

210 LCIA Arbitration Rules Art. 10(2).

211 LCIA Arbitration Rules Art. 10(3).

212 LCIA Arbitration Rules Art. 10(3).

information and supporting material from either part or any members of the tribunal including the arbitrator subject to removal.[213]

The LCIA Court may revoke the arbitrator's appointment (without reasons) if all parties agree in writing within 14 days of receipt of the written challenge statement.[214] If the parties do not agree or the challenged arbitrator does not resign, the LCIA Court shall decide whether to revoke the appointment and put its decision in writing, with reasons, and send copies to the parties, the challenged arbitrator, and the members of the tribunal.[215] A challenged arbitrator's decision to resign is not an admission of any statements within the written challenge statement.[216]

6.1.6 The Permanent Court of Arbitration

Under the PCA Arbitration Rules, an arbitrator can be challenged on grounds of independence or impartiality.[217] A party can challenge the arbitrator it previously appointed only if it becomes aware of the reasons for the challenge after the appointment is made.[218] If either party wishes to challenge an arbitrator, it must submit a notice of the challenge within 30 days of the appointment, or 30 days after learning of the circumstances that give rise to the challenge.[219] The challenge notice should specify reasons for the challenge and be communicated to other parties, the arbitrator, other members of the tribunal, and to the PCA's Secretariat, the International Bureau.[220] The other party could agree to the challenge or the arbitrator could resign his or her appointment without implying acceptance of the validity of the grounds for challenge.[221] If within 15 days from the date of notice of challenge, there is no agreement and the arbitrator has not withdrawn, the party making the challenge may ask the appointing authority to issue a decision on the challenge within 30 days from the date of notice of the challenge.[222]

Table 4 in the appendix summarizes challenges procedures.

213 LCIA Arbitration Rules Art. 10(4).
214 LCIA Arbitration Rules Art. 10(5).
215 LCIA Arbitration Rules Art. 10(6).
216 LCIA Arbitration Rules Art. 10(6).
217 PCA Arbitration Rules 2012, note 28, Art. 12(1).
218 PCA Arbitration Rules 2012, note 28, Art. 12(2).
219 PCA Arbitration Rules 2012, note 28, Art. 13(1).
220 PCA Arbitration Rules 2012, note 28, Art. 13(2).
221 PCA Arbitration Rules 2012, note 28, Art. 13(3).
222 PCA Arbitration Rules 2012, note 28, Art. 13(4).

6.2 *Reasons to Challenge*

Decisions to challenge an arbitrator are not taken lightly by the parties and their counsel.[223] Challenges can be disruptive of the entire arbitration process: they create delay and add time and cost to the proceedings and can build mistrust and increase animosity between the parties. More importantly, they also put the party in the difficult position of having to question and argue the fitness of an arbitrator to sit in the very proceedings in which they appear. It is not an enviable place to be in a dispute-resolution process. It may also create difficult dynamics with the tribunal. If the challenge is accepted, counsel will still have to appear in front of the remaining members of the original tribunal.[224] More often, as challenges are only rarely accepted, the party and its counsel will have to continue appearing before an arbitrator they have argued was unfit to hear the case. Unconscious—and unwanted—biases and resentment may linger.

Except in the rare cases in which challenges are spurious and a purely delaying tactic, therefore, a party will take the difficult decision of challenging an arbitrator only when it has a clear reason as to why the arbitrator lacks the qualities required to sit as arbitrator.[225] Challenges happen when at least one of the parties does not believe the arbitrator is independent and impartial anymore, and hence it fears the arbitrator will not give them a fair and impartial hearing.

As this section demonstrates, in practice, lack of impartiality and independence is alleged when several different situations occur. These can vary significantly and include both reasons that are pre-existing and relate to professional connections and activities and different forms of conflict, as well as reasons that develop during the course of the arbitration, including the handling of the arbitration procedure.

Reasons employed to challenge arbitrators can be broadly divided into three categories: first, and most often, there might reasons linked to professional or personal relationship between an arbitrator and a party or counsel or other relevant actor; second, there may be reasons linked to the conduct of

---

223 For an insightful view on the issue, see Andrew B. Loewenstein, *The Approach of Counsel to Challenges in International Disputes*, in GIORGETTI, CHALLENGES AND RECUSALS, *supra* note 168.

224 For a unique arbitrator prospective, see Charles N. Brower, Sarah Melikian and Michael P. Daly, *Tall and Small Tales of a Challenged Arbitrator*, in GIORGETTI, CHALLENGES AND RECUSALS, *supra* note 168.

225 On spurious and tactical challenges, *see* Constantine Partasides, *The Art of Selecting the Right Arbitrator*, Lecture at London School of Economics (Nov. 9, 2011), *available at* http://www.lse.ac.uk/newsAndMedia/videoAndAudio/channels/publicLecturesAndEvents/player.aspx?id=1252.

the arbitrator during the proceedings; and, third, there may be reasons arising from an arbitrator's alleged pre-judgment of the case—also known as issue conflicts. Each category is examined below.

6.2.1 Lack of Independence and Impartiality because of Professional or Personal Relationship between an Arbitrator and a Party or Counsel or Other Relevant Actor

The most common situations that result in the filing of an arbitrator challenge arise from some kind of professional or personal relationship between the arbitrator and some other actor in the arbitration.[226] These situations may arise because of repeat appointments, existing or past working relations, or other personal or financial relationships. More specifically, some of the reasons that resulted in the initiation of challenges proceedings include: professional relationship of the arbitrator with a party or its counsel, including multiple appointments of an arbitrator by the same party or counsel; or as a result of the merger of law firms, or the assumption of partnership or an adviser role; financial interest or link to one of the parties; the presence of a long-standing professional or personal relationship; the fact that the arbitrator and counsel previously acted as co-counsel; professional contacts between the arbitrator and counsel; family links between the arbitrator and counsel for a party; and double hatting (i.e. acting as counsel and arbitrator in related proceedings).[227]

Several examples of such situations exist. For example, in *Vito G. Gallo v. Canada*, a NAFTA case decided under UNCITRAL (1976) Rules, the claimant filed a challenge after learning the professional situation of respondent-appointed arbitrator had changed since his appointment.[228] Specifically, the arbitrator had agreed to advise Mexico, a non-disputing party under NAFTA, on general legal matters which could include international investment arbitration. The appointing authority deciding the challenge (in this case ICSID's Deputy Secretary-General) concluded that from the point of view of a "reasonable and informed third party" there would be justifiable doubts about the arbitrator's impartiality and independence. The appointing authority thus directed the arbitrator to choose whether to continue to advise Mexico, or continue to serve

226 See *generally* MARIA NICOLE CLEIS, THE INDEPENDENCE AND IMPARTIALITY OF ICSID ARBITRATORS (2017) 56–72.

227 *See generally* Meg Kinnear & Frauke Nitschke, *Disqualification of Arbitrators Under the ICSID Convention and Rules*, and Sarah Grimmer, *The Determination of Arbitrator Challenges by the Secretary-General of the Permanent Court of Arbitration* in GIORGETTI, CHALLENGES AND RECUSALS.

228 *Vito G. Gallo v. Government of Canada*, NAFTA/UNCITRAL, Decision on the Challenge to Mr. J. Christopher Thomas, QC (Oct. 14, 2009), available at http://italaw.com/documents/Gallo-Canada-Thomas_Challenge-Decision.pdf.

as an arbitrator. The arbitrator resigned from the tribunal a few days after the decision was issued.

Similarly, in *ICS v. Argentina*, another case applying UNCITRAL (1976) Rules and decided under the Argentina-United Kingdom BIT, the respondent challenged the claimant-appointed arbitrator alleging that a conflict of interest existed because the arbitrator and his firm were concurrently representing the claimant in another long-running investment treaty arbitration against Argentina.[229] The appointing authority, an individual appointed by the PCA's Secretary General under the UNCITRAL Rules, found that that the arbitrator could be considered as 'adverse' towards Argentina, a situation that was often a source of justified concerns that the appointing authority believed should in principle be avoided. The appointing authority noted that the case was not merely one in which an arbitrator's firm was acting adversely to one of the parties in the dispute, but it was a case in which the arbitrator had personally and recently acted adversely to one of the parties to the dispute.[230] He therefore held that the conflict was "sufficiently serious to give rise to objectively justifiable doubts as to [the arbitrator's] impartiality and independence."[231] The appointing authority found no reason to doubt the arbitrator's personal intention to act impartially and independently, but thought it prudent for another arbitrator to be appointed by the claimant.[232]

The question of the relationship between arbitrator and counsel was also addressed in *Blue Bank v. Venezuela*, a case filed under the Barbados—Venezuela BIT and decided under ICSID procedural rules.[233] In the case, the respondent filed a request to disqualify the claimant's appointed arbitrator[234] and the claimant filed a request to disqualify the respondent's appointed arbitrator.[235] Thus, as provided by the ICSID Rules, the Chairman of the ICSID Administrative Council decided the challenge. In its proposal for the disqualification, the respondent argued that the claimant-appointed arbitrator's interests were adverse to Venezuela's interests because the arbitrator's firm represented interests against Venezuela, and the arbitrator was a partner and

229 *ICS Inspection and Control Services Limited (United Kingdom) v. The Republic of Argentina*, UNCITRAL, PCA Case No. 2010–9, Decision on Challenge to Arbitrator, para. 1 (Dec. 17, 2009), *available at* http://italaw.com/sites/default/files/case-documents/ita0415.pdf.

230 *Id.* para. 4.

231 *Id.* para. 2.

232 *Id.* para. 5.

233 *Blue Bank International & Trust (Barbados) Ltd. v. Bolivarian Republic of Venezuela*, ICSID Case No. ARB 12/20, Decision on the Parties' Proposals to Disqualify a Majority of the Tribunal (12 Nov. 2013) at: http://www.italaw.com/cases/1513.

234 *Id.* para. 7.

235 *Id.* para. 10.

co-manager of the firm's global arbitration practice.[236] The respondent questioned in particular the arbitrator's position as a managing partner of the litigation and arbitration department at the firm's Madrid office and as member of steering committee of the firm's international dispute practice group, and the fact that the firm represented the claimant investor in another ICSID case, *Longreef v. Venezuela*, through its offices in New York and Caracas.[237] The Chairman upheld the challenge against the arbitrator on those undisputed facts and the similarity of the issues between the two ICSID cases against Venezuela, and held that a reasonable third party would find an appearance of lack of impartiality in the arbitrator's judgment.[238] The claimant's proposed disqualification of the respondent-appointed arbitrator was based on repeat appointments by Argentina and Venezuela, and on the arbitrator's alleged systematic findings in favor of respondent State.[239] The arbitrator resigned from the tribunal after submitting his remarks on the challenge[240] and the Chairman accordingly dismissed that challenge.

Repeat appointments have been the subject of several disqualification requests. In the practice of investment tribunals, what seems to matter is not the number of cases in which an arbitrator has sat, but rather how close the cases are in terms of both facts and legal issues.

In *Caratube v. Kazakhstan*, for example, the issue at stake was the similarities of two cases in which the challenged arbitrator sat and to which he was appointed by the same State.[241] In the case, Caratube and Mr. Devincci Salah Hourani, a U.S. national, filed a claim against Kazakhstan in 2013 at ICSID. In 2014, the claimants submitted a request for disqualification of the respondent-appointed arbitrator alleging he manifestly could not be "independent and impartial" because he had been appointed as arbitrator, also by Kazakhstan, in another related case, *Ruby Roz Agricol v. Kazakhstan*.[242] The claimants identified similarities between *Ruby Roz* and *Caratube* and asserted that both claims relied on essentially the same factual allegations with respect to acts and omissions and pattern of conduct. Additionally, the claimants argued that several

236 *Id.* para. 27.

237 *Id.* paras. 22–23.

238 *Id.* 66–69.

239 *Id.* paras. 45–46.

240 *Id.* para. 51.

241 *Caratube International Oil Company LLP & Mr. Devincci Salah Hourani v. Republic of Kazakhstan*, ICSID Case No. ARB/13/13, Decision on the Proposal for Disqualification of Mr. Bruno Boesch, para. 62 (Mar. 20, 2014), available at http://italaw.com/sites/default/files/case-documents/italaw3133.pdf.

242 *Ruby Roz Agricol v. Kazakhstan*, Award on Jurisdiction (UNCITRAL 2013).

individuals who submitted witness statements in *Ruby Roz* would also likely submit witness statements in *Caratube*.[243] The claimants also asserted that the same firm had appointed the same arbitrator in numerous cases, in addition to *Caratube* and *Ruby Roz*, which they feared created a potential conflict.[244]

In a first for ICSID, the two unchallenged arbitrators upheld the challenge,[245] and agreed with the claimants that *Ruby Roz* arose out of the same factual context as *Caratube* and concluded that the case exhibited an imbalance because of the respondent-appointed arbitrator's involvement with *Ruby Roz*. The two unchallenged arbitrators concluded that the challenged arbitrator could not be expected to "to maintain a 'Chinese wall' in his own mind."[246] Though they explained that they did not question his "moral character, his actual impartiality, or his honesty,[247] they concluded that "a third party would find that there is an evident or obvious appearance of lack of impartiality or independence based on a reasonable evaluation of the facts in the present case."[248] At the same time, the arbitrators found that multiple appointments by the same firm, without more, did not constitute an objective circumstance that would demonstrate the arbitrator's inability to exercise independent and impartial judgment in the case at hand.[249]

The relationship between the arbitrator and one of the parties also became the subject of a challenge in *Big Sky Energy Corporation v. Kazakhstan*, also

243 *Caratube*, supra note 241, paras. 24–26.
244 *Id.* para. 30.
245 *Id.* para. 111.
246 *Id.* para. 75.
247 *Id.* para. 64.
248 *Id.* para. 91.
249 *Id.* para. 109. (also holding at para. 107 that "The Unchallenged Arbitrators agree with the two remaining arbitrators in *Tidewater* that the mere fact of Mr. Boesch's prior appointments as arbitrator by Curtis, Mallet-Prevost, Colt & Mosle LLP, one of which was made on behalf of the Respondent in the Ruby Roz arbitration, does not, without more, indicate a manifest lack of independence or impartiality on the part of Mr. Boesch. Absent any other objective circumstances demonstrating that these prior appointments manifestly influence his ability to exercise independent judgment in the present arbitration, they do not on their own justify Mr. Boesch's disqualification" and nonetheless observing at para. 108 that "Be it only said that the Unchallenged Arbitrators are impressed in particular by the fact that there exists a sufficient number of potential arbitrators for an appointment to be made without any appearance being given of an existing link, real or suspected, between the arbitrator and the appointing party and its counsel. And conversely, that it is quite natural that a party and its counsel will wish to appoint the "best" arbitrator available for a given case and that prior experiences with that potential arbitrator are of course adequate to give that assurance".).

an ICSID case.[250] The claimant, a US investor, filed a proposal for disqualification of the respondent- appointed arbitrator arguing that the arbitrator's past professional ties to members of the Kazakh judiciary put in question his impartiality and independence in the eyes of an independent third-party. These ties rose out of his previous employment by the German Office of International Cooperation, through which he had participated in a project for legal and judicial reform in various newly independent Central Asian states, including Kazakhstan.[251] The proposal for disqualification was upheld by the two remaining co-arbitrators, who decided the challenge under the applicable ICSID Rules.

In a more recent case, the President of an ICSID tribunal was challenged because of her husband's work on behalf of the respondent, Colombia, in an unrelated matter at the International Court of Justice.[252] She resigned before the challenge was decided.[253]

This case also serves to highlight an important epiphenomenon of challenges: often an arbitrator will resign before a decision is taken on the validity of the challenge. Resignations may be prompted by diverse reasons: the desire of the arbitrator not to disrupt the proceedings, the unwillingness to go through the challenge proceeding, or a possible agreement with the substance of the challenge. It is thus important to recognize that resignation pre-challenge decision may skew the analysis of challenges procedures and their results.

6.2.2 Lack of Independence and Impartiality because of Conduct of the Arbitrator during the Proceedings or that Arose during the Proceedings

Challenges may also be brought for reasons linked to the conduct of arbitrators during proceedings or prior to the commencement of proceedings, including

---

250 *Big Sky Energy Corporation v. Republic of Kazakhstan*, ICSID Case No. ARB/17/22, Decision on the Disqualification Proposal of Mr Rolf Knieper, May 3, 2018, procedural details are available at: https://icsid.worldbank.org/en/Pages/cases/casedetail.aspx?CaseNo=ARB/17/22.

251 Global Arbitration Review, *Arbitrator Disqualified Over Ties to Kazakh Judges*, https://globalarbitrationreview.com/article/1169202/arbitrator-disqualified-over-ties-to-kazakh-judges (last visited Dec. 21, 2018) (the decision itself is not public).

252 *Gran Colombia Gold Corp. v. Republic of Colombia* (ICSID Case No. ARB/18/23), the proposal for disqualification was filed on January 4, 2019 and the President resigned on February 5, 2019. Information on the case are available at: https://icsid.worldbank.org/en/Pages/cases/casedetail.aspx?CaseNo=ARB/18/23.

253 *Malintoppi resigns after challenge over husband's counsel work*, Feb. 6, 2019, Global Arbitration Review, https://globalarbitrationreview.com/article/1180057/malintoppi-resigns-after-challenge-over-husband's-counsel-work.

for claims of financial dependence, failure to disclose a conflict, or failure to act.

The *Burlington v. Republic of Ecuador* case tackled issues concerning repeat appointments of the same arbitrator by counsel, duties of disclosure, as well as arbitrator conduct during proceedings. The case, applying ICSID rules under the Ecuador—United States BIT, was decided by the Chairman of ICSID's Administrative Council after the two remaining co-arbitrators failed to reach a decision on the challenge.[254] Several years after the beginning of the proceedings, counsel for the respondent learnt from news report that claimant-appointed arbitrator had been appointed as arbitrator multiple times by counsel acting for the claimant. It thus asked the arbitrator to disclose all of his appointments in cases with the same counsel, and particularly any cases accepted after signing his disclosure declaration as well as compensation paid in those cases.[255] Proceedings in the main case were suspended and challenge proceedings were initiated, in which all parties, including the challenged arbitrator, were given the opportunity to provide written statements, and as a result of which the respondent learnt that the arbitrator had been nominated by the claimant's counsel eight times.

On the issue of multiple appointments and the duty of disclosure, the Chairman of ICSID's Administrative Council found that the respondent had had sufficient information to file its disqualification proposal "on the basis of repeat appointments and non-disclosure of such appointments well before it did" and thus held those issues were time-barred.[256]

However, the Chairman found that the issue of the arbitrator's conduct during proceedings had been timely raised. On this issue the Chairman analyzed in particular the following paragraph in the arbitrator's written statement:

> Lastly there are some ethical assertions that cannot be left unanswered. [Respondent's counsel] admonishes this arbitrator to resign on ethical grounds as if [respondent's counsel's] views were proven correct. This is certainly not the case. Moreover, the real ethical question seems to lie with [respondent's counsel's] submissions and the handling of confidential information. To the best of this arbitrator's knowledge the correspondence concerning disclosure and other matters in *Pan American v. Bolivia* is part of the confidential record of that case. [Respondent's counsel] is in the knowledge of such correspondence as counsel for Bolivia, but it does not seem appropriate or ethically justified that this information be

254 *Id.* para. 16.
255 *Id.* para. 4.
256 *Id.* para. 75.

> now used to the advantage of a different client of [respondent's counsel], a use that in any event should be consented to by the other party to that case.[257]

The Chairman found that in his reply to the challenge, the arbitrator had made comments that did "not serve any purpose in addressing the proposal for disqualification" or explaining relevant circumstances.[258] He thus decided to uphold the challenge finding that a third party undertaking a reasonable evaluation of this statement would conclude it "manifestly evidences an appearance of lack of impartiality" with respect to Ecuador and its counsel.[259]

In sum, arbitrator conduct vis-à-vis the parties is relevant both within and outside the arbitral proceedings and reasons for challenges can be created at any time including after the commencement of the arbitration.

6.2.3 Lack of Independence and Impartiality because of Pre-Judgment: Issue Conflicts

Past decisions, academic writings or other public statements authored by an arbitrator may also give rise to concerns that the arbitrator does not come to the case with an open mind, and that the arbitrator has prejudged an issue that is important in the instant proceedings.

In such cases, the alleged lack of impartiality and independence is due to an "issue conflict".

In the ICSID case *Urbaser v. Argentina*, for example, Claimants challenged the appointment of Respondent-appointed arbitrator because of the views he had expressed in his scholarly publications on two questions Claimants considered crucial to the arbitration.[260] Claimants alleged that arbitrator had prejudged essential elements of the dispute that was the object of the arbitration.[261] However, the two unchallenged arbitrators differed and held that the scholarly opinions expressed by the challenged arbitrator did not meet the threshold of "presenting an appearance" that he would not be prepared to hear and consider the position of the parties "with full independence and impartiality."[262]

---

257 *Id.*

258 *Id.* para. 79.

259 *Id.* para. 80.

260 *Urbaser S.A. and Consorcio de Aguas Bilbao Bizkaia, Bilbao Biskaia Ur Partzuergoa v. The Argentine Republic*, ICSID Case No. ARB/07/26, Decision on Claimants' Proposal to Disqualify Professor Campbell McLachlan, Arbitrator, para. 20 (Aug. 12, 2010) available at: www.italaw.com/sites/default/files/case-documents/ita0887.pdf.

261 *Id.* paras. 23–24.

262 *Id.* para. 58.

Issue conflict was also addressed in the seminal *Devas v. India*, a case brought under the India—Mauritius BIT and applying the UNICTRAL (1976) Rules.[263] Respondent challenged the arbitrator appointed by claimant as well as the Presiding Arbitrator. The challenge was decided by the President of the International Court of Justice, Judge Peter Tomka, as the appointing authority under the applicable rules. Respondent argued that the two challenged arbitrators "strongly held and articulated positions" in the case on a controversial legal standard which would give rise to justifiable doubt as to their impartiality.[264] Specifically, Respondent referred to decisions by three ICSID tribunals chaired by Claimant-appointed arbitrator, and in two of which the Presiding Arbitrator served as an co-arbitrator, as well a chapter in a book written by Claimant-appointed arbitrator after the decisions were issued in which he reiterated his position on the legal question at issue (the question of "essential security interest").[265] President Tomka first noted that it was not surprising that the two challenged arbitrators had decided consistently in the ICSID cases because those tribunals had applied the same provision to similar facts.[266] President Tomka then specifically assessed the relevance of the chapter written by Claimant-appointed arbitrator and concluded that it showed that

> his view remained unchanged. Would a reasonable observer believe that the respondent has a chance to convince him to change his mind on the same legal concept? [Claimant-appointed arbitrator] is certainly entitled to his views, including to his academic freedom. But equally the respondent is entitled to have its arguments heard and ruled upon by arbitrators with an open mind. Here, the right of the latter has to prevail.[267]

For that reason, he upheld the disqualification request of Claimant-appointed arbitrator, while he rejected the disqualification proposal of the Presiding Arbitrator.[268]

---

263 *CC/Devas (Mauritius) Ltd., Devas Employees Mauritius Private Limited and Telecom Devas Mauritius Limited v. India*, UNCITRAL, Decision on the Respondent's Challenge to the Hon. Marc Lalonde and Prof. Francisco Orrego Vicuña (30 Sept. 2013), available at: http://www.italaw.com/sites/default/files/case-documents/italaw3161.pdf.pdf.

264 *Id.* para. 17.

265 *Id.* paras. 19 and 22.

266 *Id.* para. 59.

267 *Id.* para. 64.

268 *Id.* paras. 64, 66–67. On this decision, see in general, Romain Zamour, *Issue Conflicts and the Reasonable Expectation of an Open Mind: The Challenge Decision in Devas v. India and its Impact* in GIORGETTI, CHALLENGES AND RECUSALS, *supra* note 168.

7 Replacement of the Arbitrator

Challenge proceedings may result in the disqualification of an arbitrator and thus result in the creation of a vacancy on the arbitral tribunal. Vacancies may arise for other reasons also, including the resignation or death of an arbitrator. In general, the new appointment is made in the same way as the original appointment.

For example, ICSID provides that after a tribunal is constituted and proceedings have begun, the composition of the tribunal should remain unchanged, unless the death, incapacitation or resignation of an arbitrator results in the vacancy of the tribunals. Such vacancies are filled in accordance with the provisions applicable for the nomination of arbitrators.[269]

Similarly, under UNCITRAL Rules, if an arbitrator has to be replaced during the course of the proceedings, the substitute arbitration is to be appointed pursuant to the procedure that was applicable to the appointment of choice of the arbitrator being replaced.[270]

Note, however, that the ICC Rules afford the Court the discretion to decide whether or not to follow the original nominating process.[271]

The replacement of an arbitrator may be disruptive, and it is all the more disruptive the closer it gets to the end of proceedings.[272] For this reason, the

269 ICSID Convention, Art. 56.

270 UNCITRAL Rules (2010), Art. 14 (stating that "Subject to paragraph 2, in any event where an arbitrator has to be replaced during the course of the arbitral proceedings, a substitute arbitrator shall be appointed or chosen pursuant to the procedure provided for in articles 8 to 11 that was applicable to the appointment or choice of the arbitrator being replaced. This procedure shall apply even if during the process of appointing the arbitrator to be replaced, a party had failed to exercise its right to appoint or to participate in the appointment."); *see also* SCC Rules, Art. 17 ("The Board shall appoint a new arbitrator where an arbitrator has been released from his/her appointment pursuant to Article 16 (release of appointment), or where an arbitrator has died. If the arbitrator being replaced was appointed by a party, that party shall appoint the new arbitrator, unless otherwise deemed appropriate by the Board.").

271 ICC Rules, Art. 15(4) (stating: "When an arbitrator is to be replaced, the Court has discretion to decide whether or not to follow the original nominating process. Once reconstituted, and after having invited the parties to comment, the arbitral tribunal shall determine if and to what extent prior proceedings shall be repeated before the reconstituted arbitral tribunal.").

272 On the important topic of resignation, *see* Judith Levine, *Late-in-the-Day Arbitrator Challenges and Resignations: Anecdotes and Antidotes*, in GIORGETTI, CHALLENGES AND RECUSALS, *supra* note 168.

appointing authority may authorize a truncated tribunal to proceed with the finalization of the proceedings.[273]

8 Conclusion

The selection of arbitrators is an essential component of international investment arbitration.

In a system that—so far—allows the parties to select one or more of the arbitrators that will decide the case, appointing the "right" arbitrator becomes essential. Counsel and their clients spend considerable time and resources researching arbitrators and delving into their professional, personal and academic history. Resources and databases for such research are becoming more common.[274]

This book aims at explaining critically the selection of arbitrators both substantively and procedurally.

In its second part, the book also assesses arbitrator challenges by first focusing on the procedure and then analysis the available case-law. This is also a crucial issue, which is gaining increasing attention.

At the time of writing, the practice of party-appointment of arbitrators is under increased scrutiny. The main changes occurring under UNCITRAL and ICSID have been taken into consideration as much as possible in this draft. We seem to be at a pivotal moment.

Some of the criticisms are apposite. Problems such as lack of diversity and repeat appointments are systemic, and the future viability of the system will turn in part on how they will be addressed. As the interest for ISDS in the general public increase, the system of ISDS itself must take into consideration and respond to calls for more transparency and reform. In this vein, the proposal of the European Commission that an investment court is established and arbitrators are replaced by permanent judges will create a completely new model. As such, the mere proposal itself has generated interesting debate and welcomed introspection.

---

273 UNICTRAL Rules 2010 provide for that situation. See generally Brook Daly, *Permanent Court of Arbitration*, in C. GIORGETTI, RULES AND PRACTICE OF INTERNATIONAL COURTS AND TRIBUNALS, *supra* note 168.

274 *See, e.g.*, https://icsid.worldbank.org/en/Pages/arbitrators/CVSearch.aspx, Arbitrator Intelligence database available at: https://www.arbitratorintelligence.org, and effort in the Global Arbitration Review (GAR).

Appendix

TABLE 1 Selection of arbitrators: Applicable provisions

Institution	Regular rules	Default rules	Arbitrators selection method
International Center for Settlement of Investment Disputes (ICSID)	If the parties did not agree on the number of arbitrators and the method of arbitrator appointment: the party that initiated the request for the arbitration has ten days after the registration of said request to propose to the other party the appointment of one sole arbitrator or a specified uneven number of arbitrators and also specify the proposed method of appointment. The other party then has twenty days after receipt of the proposal to either accept the proposal or make a counter proposal. The first party then has twenty days to confirm or reject the counter proposal.[a] The communications described in this procedure has to be made in writing and shall be transmitted either through ICSID's Secretary-General or between the parties with a copy provided to the	If ninety days or more have passed since the request for the arbitration is registered and no agreement was made either party may ask the Chairman of the administrative council of ICSID to appoint the missing arbitrators[j] and to designate a President of the tribunal.[k] The Secretary-General then sends a copy of the request to the other party.[l] The Chairman shall consult both parties, as possible, and use his or her best effort to make a selection within thirty days.[m] The Secretary-General shall then notify the parties of the chairman's selection or designation.[n] If the parties agreed that the arbitrators shall elect a President of the tribunal and the selected arbitrators fail to do so: either party may write to the	Arbitrators may be appointed from outside the Panel of Arbitrators,[q] except in the case of appointmen by the Chairman of the administrative council of ICSID.[r] The Centre shall have a Administrative Council and a Secretariat and shall maintain a Panel o Conciliators and a Pane of Arbitrators.[s] The Panel of Conciliato and the Panel of Arbitrators shall each consist of qualified persons, designated as hereinafter provided, who are willing to serve thereon.[t] Each Contracting State may designate to each Panel four persons who may but need not be its nationals.[u] The Chairman may desi nate ten persons to eac Panel. The persons

TABLE 1 Selection of arbitrators: Applicable provisions (*cont.*)

stitution	Regular rules	Default rules	Arbitrators selection method
	Secretary-General. The Secretary-General should be notified by the parties as soon as an agreement is reached.[b] If sixty days or more have passed since the request for the arbitration is registered and no agreement was made: either party may inform the Secretary-General that it intends to follow the formula specified in Article 37(2)(b) of the convention. Then, the Secretary-General informs the other party that the tribunal is to be composed in this method.[c] Article 37(2)(b) provides that the tribunal consist of "three arbitrators, one arbitrator appointed by each party and the third, who shall be the president of the Tribunal, appointed by agreement of the parties."[d] If Article 37(2)(b) formula is to be followed, then, in a communication	Chairman of the administrative council to ask the Chairman to appoint a President of the tribunal.[o] Parties are to notify the Secretary-General of the appointment of each arbitrator and specify the method of appointment. Then, the Secretary-General seeks acceptance from the appointee. If a selected arbitrator fails to accept appointment within fifteen days, the Secretary-General notifies the parties and invites them to appoint another arbitrator using the same method.[p]	so designated to a Panel shall each have a different nationality.[v] Persons designated to serve on the Panels shall be persons of high moral character and recognized competence in the fields of law, commerce, industry or finance, who may be relied upon to exercise independent judgment. Competence in the field of law shall be of particular importance in the case of persons on the Panel of Arbitrators.[w] The Chairman, in designating persons to serve on the Panels, shall in addition pay due regard to the importance of assuring representation on the Panels of the principal legal systems of the world and of the main forms of economic activity.[x] Panel members shall serve for renewable periods of six years.[y]

TABLE 1 Selection of arbitrators: Applicable provisions (*cont.*)

Institution	Regular rules	Default rules	Arbitrators selection method
	to the other party, either party names two persons, identifying one as "the arbitrator appointed by it" who should not be of the same nationality as either of the parties, and identify the other person as "the arbitrator proposed to be the President of the Tribunal" and invite the other party to "concur in the appointment of the arbitrator proposed to be the President of the tribunal and to appoint another arbitrator".[e] The other party shall promptly reply naming the arbitrator to be appointed by it who should not be of the same nationality as either of the parties, and either concur the appointment of the proposed president or name another person as the arbitrator proposed to be the President of the tribunal.[f] The first party shall then notify the second party whether it concurs the appointment of the arbitrator proposed to be the President of		In case of death or resignation of a membe of a Panel, the authority which designated the member shall have the right to designate another person to serve for the remainder of tha member's term.[z] Panel members shall co tinue in office until thei successors have been designated.[aa] A person may serve on both Panels.[ab] If a person shall have been designated to serve on the same Panel by more than one Contracting State, or by one or more Contractin States and the Chairma he shall be deemed to have been designated by the authority which first designated him or, if one such authority is the State of which he is national, by that State.[a] All designations shall b notified to the Secretary General and shall take

TABLE 1 Selection of arbitrators: Applicable provisions (*cont.*)

stitution	Regular rules	Default rules	Arbitrators selection method
	the tribunal.[g] The communications described in this procedure has to be made in writing and shall be transmitted either through ICSID's Secretary-General or between the parties with a copy provided to the Secretary-General.[h] Annulment: 52(3) On receipt of the request [for annulment] the Chairman shall forthwith appoint from the Panel of Arbitrators an ad hoc Committee of three persons. None of the members of the Committee shall have been a member of the Tribunal which rendered the award, shall be of the same nationality as any such member, shall be a national of the State party to the dispute or of the state whose national is a party to the dispute, shall have been designated to the Panel of Arbitrators by either of those states, or shall have acted as a conciliator in the same dispute.[i]		effect from the date on which the notification is received.[ad] Arbitrators appointed by the Chairman shall not be nationals of the contracting state party to the dispute.[ae]

TABLE 1 Selection of arbitrators: Applicable provisions (*cont.*)

Institution	Regular rules	Default rules	Arbitrators selection method
UN Commission on International Trade Law (UNCITRAL)[af]	If the parties have agreed that a sole arbitrator is to be appointed and if within 30 days after receipt by all other parties of a proposal for the appointment of a sole arbitrator, the parties have not reached agreement thereon: – a sole arbitrator shall, at the request of a party, be appointed by the appointing authority.[ag]	If for any reason the appointment cannot be made according to the list procedure of Art. 8, the appointing authority may exercise its discretion in appointing the sole arbitrator.[ah]	The appointing authorit shall use the following list-procedure, unless the parties agree that the list-procedure should not be used or unless the appointing authority determines in its discretion that the use of the list-procedure is not appropriate for the case: – The appointing authority shall communicate to each of the parties an identic list containing at leas three names; – Within 15 days after the receipt of this list each party may returr the list to the appoint ing authority after hav ing deleted the name or names to which it objects and numbere the remaining names on the list in the orde of its preference; After the expiration of the above period of tim the appointing authorit shall appoint the sole ar bitrator from among the names approved on the

TABLE 1 Selection of arbitrators: Applicable provisions (*cont.*)

itution	Regular rules	Default rules	Arbitrators selection method
			lists returned to it and in accordance with the order of preference indicated by the parties;[ai]
	If three arbitrators are to be appointed: – each party shall appoint one arbitrator. The two arbitrators thus appointed shall choose the third arbitrator who will act as the presiding arbitrator of the arbitral tribunal.[aj] and if there were there are multiple parties as claimant or as respondent and parties have agreed to another method of appointment of arbitrators the multiple parties jointly, whether as claimant or as respondent, shall appoint an arbitrator.[ak] If the parties have agreed that the arbitral tribunal is to be composed of a number of arbitrators other than one or three:	If within 30 days after the receipt of a party's notification of the appointment of an arbitrator, the other party has not notified the first party of the arbitrator it has appointed: – the first party may request the appointing authority to appoint the second arbitrator.[am] – If within 30 days after the appointment of the second arbitrator the two arbitrators have not agreed on the choice of the presiding arbitrator: the presiding arbitrator shall be appointed by the appointing authority in the same way as a sole arbitrator would be appointed under article 8.[an]	In the event of any failure to constitute the arbitral tribunal under these Rules: – the appointing authority shall, at the request of any party, constitute the arbitral tribunal and, in doing so, may revoke any appointment already made and appoint or reappoint each of the arbitrators and designate one of them as the presiding arbitrator.[ao]

TABLE 1 Selection of arbitrators: Applicable provisions (*cont.*)

Institution	Regular rules	Default rules	Arbitrators selec method
	the arbitrators shall be appointed according to the method agreed upon by the parties.[al]		
Permanent Court of Arbitration (PCA)	Unless the parties have agreed on the number of arbitrators previously, and if within 30 days after the receipt by the respondent of the notice of arbitration the parties have not agreed on the number of arbitrators, three arbitrators shall be appointed.[ap]	If no other parties have responded to a party's proposal to appoint a sole arbitrator within these 30 days, and the party or parties concerned have failed to appoint a second arbitrator, a party may request the appointing authority to appoint a sole arbitrator and it may do so if it determines that it is appropriate.[aq] If the parties have previously agreed to appoint a sole arbitrator and did not reach an agreement within 30 days, either party may request the appointing authority to appoint a sole arbitrator.[ar]	As soon as possib appointing autho shall make the appointment usi procedure: a) Th appointing autho sends a list conta least three name of the parties; b) party, within 15 may privately se the list back to th appointing autho after deleting the to which it objec and numbering t remaining name the order of its preference; c) aft 15 days, the appo authority shall appoint the sole arbitrator from a the names appro the lists returned and in accordan the order of pref indicated by the d) If for any reas appointment car

TABLE 1 Selection of arbitrators: Applicable provisions (*cont.*)

stitution	Regular rules	Default rules	Arbitrators selection method
			be made according to this procedure, the appointing authority may exercise its discretion in appointing the sole arbitrator.[as] The appointing authority could determine the list procedure is not appropriate for a specific case.[at]
	Parties may agree on the number and procedure for appointment of the Arbitral Tribunal.[au] – If the parties do not agree on a number, the Board decides.[av] – Where the Arbitral Tribunal is to consist of a sole arbitrator: the parties shall be given 10 days to jointly appoint the arbitrator. – Where the Arbitral Tribunal is to consist of more than one arbitrator: each party shall appoint an equal number of arbitrators and the Board shall appoint the Chairperson.	If the parties have not agreed on a procedure, or the Arbitral Tribunal has not been appointed within the time period agreed by the parties or, the parties have not agreed on a time period, within the time period set by the Board:[aw] If the parties fail to appoint the arbitrator(s) within this time, the Board shall make the appointment.[ax] In case of multiple parties, if either side fails to make such joint appointment, the Board may appoint the entire Arbitral Tribunal.[ay]	If the parties fail to appoint the arbitrator within this time, the Board shall make the appointment. If the two arbitrators did not agree on presiding arbitrator, then the presiding arbitrator shall be appointed by the appointing authority in the same way as a sole arbitrator would be appointed If the parties are of different nationalities: – the sole arbitrator or the Chairperson of the Arbitral Tribunal shall be of a different nationality than the parties, unless the

TABLE 1 Selection of arbitrators: Applicable provisions (*cont.*)

Institution	Regular rules	Default rules	Arbitrators selection method
Stockholm Chamber of Commerce (SCC)	– Where there are multiple claimants or respondents and the Arbitral Tribunal is to consist of more than one arbitrator: the multiple claimants, jointly, and the multiple respondents, jointly, shall appoint an equal number of arbitrators.		parties have agreed otherwise, or the Board otherwise deems it appropriate.[az] – When appointing arbitrators, the Board shall consider the nature and circumstances of the dispute, the applicable law, the seat and language of the arbitration and the nationality of the parties.[ba]
London Court of International Arbitration (LCIA)	No party or third person may appoint any arbitrator under the Arbitration Agreement. The LCIA Court alone is empowered to appoint arbitrators (albeit taking into account any written agreement or joint nomination by the parties).[bb] The LCIA Court shall appoint the Arbitral Tribunal promptly after receipt by the Registrar of the Response or, if no Response is received, after 35 days from the	If the parties have agreed that the claimant or the respondent or any third person (other than the LCIA Court) is to nominate an arbitrator and such nomination is not made within time or at all (in the Request, Response or otherwise): – the LCIA Court may appoint an arbitrator notwithstanding any absent or late nomination.[bf] In the absence of written agreement between the Parties, no party may	The President of the LCIA Court shall only be eligible to be appointed as an arbitrator if the parties agree in writing to nominate him or her as the sole or presiding arbitrator; and the Vice Presidents of the LCIA Court and the Chairman of the LCIA Board of Directors (the latter being ex officio a member of the LCIA Court) shall only be eligible to be appointed as arbitrators if nominated in writing by a party or parties—provided that no such

TABLE 1 Selection of arbitrators: Applicable provisions (*cont.*)

stitution	Regular rules	Default rules	Arbitrators selection method
	Commencement Date (or such other lesser or greater period to be determined by the LCIA Court pursuant to Article 22.5).[bc] A sole arbitrator shall be appointed unless the parties have agreed in writing otherwise or if the LCIA Court determines that in the circumstances a three-member tribunal is appropriate (or, exceptionally, more than three).[bd] If the parties agreed that any arbitrator is to be appointed by one or more of them or by any third person (other than the LCIA Court): – that agreement shall be treated under the Arbitration Agreement as an agreement to nominate an arbitrator for all purposes. Such nominee may only be appointed by the LCIA Court as arbitrator subject to that nominee's compliance with	unilaterally nominate a sole arbitrator or presiding arbitrator.[bg] If the Arbitration Agreement entitles each party to nominate an arbitrator: the parties to the dispute number more than two and such parties have not all agreed in writing that the disputant parties represent collectively two separate "sides" for the formation of the Arbitral Tribunal (as Claimants on one side and Respondents on the other side, each side nominating a single arbitrator), the LCIA Court shall appoint the Arbitral Tribunal without regard to any party's entitlement or nomination.[bh] In such circumstances, the Arbitration Agreement shall be treated for all purposes as a written agreement by the parties for the nomination and	nominee shall have taken or shall take thereafter any part in any function of the LCIA Court or LCIA relating to such arbitration.[bj] Before appointment by the LCIA Court, each arbitral candidate shall furnish to the Registrar (upon the latter's request) a brief written summary of his or her qualifications and professional positions (past and present); the candidate shall also agree in writing fee-rates conforming to the Schedule of Costs; the candidate shall sign a written declaration stating: (i) whether there are any circumstances currently known to the candidate which are likely to give rise in the mind of any party to any justifiable doubts as to his or her impartiality or independence and, if so, specifying in full such circumstances in the declaration; and (ii) whether the candidate

TABLE 1 Selection of arbitrators: Applicable provisions (*cont.*)

Institution	Regular rules	Default rules	Arbitrators selection method
	Articles 5.3 to 5.5; and the LCIA Court shall refuse to appoint any nominee if it determines that the nominee is not so compliant or is otherwise unsuitable.[be]	appointment of the Arbitral Tribunal by the LCIA Court alone.[bi]	is ready, willing and abl[e] to devote sufficient time diligence and industry t[o] ensure the expeditious and efficient conduct of the arbitration. The candidate shall furnish promptly such agreeme[nt] and declaration to the Registrar.[bk]
International Chamber of Commerce (ICC)	The disputes shall be decided by a sole arbitrator or by three arbitrators.[bl] If parties have not agreed upon the number of arbitrators: – the Court shall appoint a sole arbitrator, save where it appears to the Court that the dispute is such as to warrant the appointment of three arbitrators.[bm] – In such case, the claimant shall nominate an arbitrator within a period of 15 days from the receipt of the notification of the decision of the Court, and the respondent shall nominate an arbitrator within a period	In the absence of a joint nomination pursuant to Articles 12(6) or 12(7) and where all parties are unable to agree to a method for the constitution of the arbitral tribunal, the Court may appoint each member of the arbitral tribunal and shall designate one of them to act as president. In such case, the Court shall be at liberty to choose any person it regards as suitable to act as arbitrator, applying Article 13 when it considers this appropriate.[bu] Confirmation shall be reported to the Court at its next session. If	Where the Court is to appoint an arbitrator, it shall make the appointment upon proposal of a National Committee or Group of the ICC that it considers to be appropriate.[bx] If the Court does not accept the proposal made, or if the National Committee or Group fai[ls] to make the proposal requested within the time limit fixed by the Court: – the Court may repeat its request, request a proposal from anoth[er] National Committee or Group that it considers to be appropriate, or appoint directly any person

TABLE 1 Selection of arbitrators: Applicable provisions (*cont.*)

stitution	Regular rules	Default rules	Arbitrators selection method
	of 15 days from the receipt of the notification of the nomination made by the claimant. If a party fails to nominate an arbitrator, the appointment shall be made by the Court.[bn] If Sole Arbitrator is to be nominated, Parties may, by agreement, nominate the sole arbitrator for confirmation.[bo] If three arbitrators are to be nominated, each party shall nominate in the Request and the Answer, respectively, one arbitrator for confirmation.[bp] – the third arbitrator, who will act as president of the arbitral tribunal, shall be appointed by the Court[bq] – if the parties have agreed upon another procedure for such appointment, in which case the nomination will be subject to confirmation pursuant to Article 13.[br]	the Secretary General considers that a co-arbitrator, sole arbitrator or president of an arbitral tribunal should not be confirmed, the matter shall be submitted to the Court. If the parties fail to nominate a sole arbitrator within 30 days from the date when the claimant's Request for Arbitration has been received by the other party, or within such additional time as may be allowed by the Secretariat, the sole arbitrator shall be appointed by the Court.[bv] If a party fails to nominate an arbitrator, the appointment shall be made by the Court.[bw] If the parties have agree on another procedure and when such procedure not result in a nomination within 30 days from the confirmation or appointment of the co-arbitrators or any	whom it regards as suitable.[by] – The Court may also appoint directly to act as arbitrator any person whom it regards as suitable where: – one or more of the parties is a state or may be considered to be a state entity; – the Court considers that it would be appropriate to appoint an arbitrator from a country or territory where there is no National Committee or Group; or the President certifies to the Court that circumstances exist which, in the President's opinion, make a direct appointment necessary and appropriate.[bz]

TABLE 1 Selection of arbitrators: Applicable provisions (*cont.*)

Institution	Regular rules	Default rules	Arbitrators selection method
		other time limit agreed by the parties or fixed by the Court, the third arbitrator shall be appointed by the Court.	
	Where there are multiple claimants or multiple respondents, and where the dispute is to be referred to three arbitrators, the multiple claimants, jointly, and the multiple respondents, jointly, shall nominate an arbitrator for confirmation pursuant to Article 13.[bs] Where an additional party has been joined, and where the dispute is to be referred to three arbitrators, the additional party may, jointly with the claimant(s) or with the respondent(s), nominate an arbitrator for confirmation pursuant to Article 13.[bt]		

a ICSID Rules, *supra* note 18, Rule 2(1).
b *Id.*, Rule 2(2).
c *Id.*, Rule 2(3).
d *Id.*, Art. 40(1).
e *Id.*, Rule 3(1)(a).
f *Id.*, Rule 3(1)(b).
g *Id.*, Rule 3(1)(c).
h *Id.*, Rule 3(2).

i ICSID Convention, Art. 52(3).
j ICSID Rules *Id.*, Art. 38.
k *Id.*, Rule 4(1).
l *Id.*, Rule 4(3).
m *Id.*, Rule 4(4).
n *Id.*, Rule 4(5).
o *Id.*, Rule 4(2).
p *Id.*, Rule 5.
q *Id.*, Art. 40(2).
r *Id.*, Art. 40(1).
s *Id.*, Art. 3.
t *Id.*, Art. 12.
u *Id.*, Art. 13(1).
v *Id.*, Art. 13(2).
w *Id.*, Art. 14(1).
x *Id.*, Art. 14(2).
y *Id.*, Art. 15(1).
z *Id.*, Art. 15(2).
aa *Id.*, Art. 15(3).
ab *Id.*, Art. 16(1).
ac *Id.*, Art. 16(2).
ad *Id.*, Art. 16(3).
ae *Id.*, Art. 38.
af UNCITRAL Arbitration Rules as revised in 2013, G.A. Res. 68/109, 68th Sess., U.N. Doc. A/RES/68/109 (Dec. 16, 2013), available at http://www.uncitral.org/pdf/english/texts/arbitration/arb-rules-2013/UNCITRAL-Arbitration-Rules-2013-e.pdf [hereinafter UNCITRAL Rules].
ag *Id.*, Art. 8(1).
ah *Id.*, Art. 8.2(d).
ai *Id.*, Art. 8.2.
aj *Id.*, Art. 9(1).
ak *Id.*, Art. 10(1).
al *Id.*, Art. 10(2).
am *Id.*, Art. 9(2).
an *Id.*, Art. 9(3).
ao *Id.*, Art. 10(3).
ap Permanent Court of Arbitration—Arbitration Rules 2012, (Dec. 17, 2012), available at https://pca-cpa.org/wp-content/uploads/sites/175/2015/11/PCA-Arbitration-Rules-2012.pdf [hereinafter PCA Arbitration Rules 2012]. Art. 7(1).
aq *Id.*, Art. 7(2).
ar *Id.*, Art. 8(1).
as *Id.*, Art. 8(2).
at *Id.*, Art. 8(2).
au Arbitration Rules of the Arbitration Institute of the Stockholm Chamber of Commerce, (Jan 1, 2017), available at https://sccinstitute.com/media/293614/arbitration_rules_eng_17_web.pdf [hereinafter SCC Arbitration Rules 2017]. Art. 17 (1).
av *Id.*, Art. 16.
aw *Id.*, Art. 17 (2).

ax *Id.*, Art. 17(3) and (4).
ay *Id.*, Art. 17 (5).
az *Id.*, Art. 17 (6).
ba *Id.*, Art. 17 (7).
bb London Court of International Arbitration, (Oct. 1, 2014), available at http://www.lcia.org/dispute_resolution_services/lcia-arbitration-rules-2014.aspx [hereinafter LCIA Arbitration Rules 2014]. Art 5(7).
bc *Id.*, Art 5(8).
bd *Id.*, Art 5(6).
be *Id.*, Art 7(1).
bf *Id.*, Art 7(2).
bg *Id.*, Art 7(3).
bh *Id.*, Art 8(1).
bi *Id.*, Art 8(2).
bj *Id.*, Art 5(10).
bk *Id.*, Art. 5(4).
bl International Chamber of Commerce Rules of Arbitration, (Mar. 1, 2017), available at https://cdn.iccwbo.org/content/uploads/sites/3/2017/01/ICC-2017-Arbitration-and-2014-Mediation-Rules-english-version.pdf.pdf [hereinafter ICC Arbitration Rules 2017]. Art. 12(1).
bm *Id.*, Art. 12(2).
bn *Id.*, Art. 12(2).
bo *Id.*, Art. 12(3).
bp *Id.*, Art. 12(4).
bq *Id.*, Art. 12(5).
br *Id.*, Art. 12(5).
bs *Id.*, Art. 12(6).
bt *Id.*, Art. 12(7).
bu *Id.*, Art. 12(8).
bv *Id.*, Art. 12(3).
bw *Id.*, Art. 12(4).
bx *Id.*, Art 13(3).
by *Id.*, Art 13(3).
bz *Id.*, Art 13(4).

TABLE 2 Selection of arbitrators: Rules & obligations of appointing authorities

stitution	Rules	Requirements
SID	Article 38: If the Tribunal has not been constituted within 90 days after notice of registration of the request has been dispatched by the Secretary-General in accordance with paragraph (3) of Article 36, or such other period as the parties may agree, the Chairman shall, at the request of either party and after consulting both parties as far as possible, appoint the arbitrator or arbitrators not yet appointed. Arbitrators appointed by the Chairman pursuant to this Article shall not be nationals of the Contracting State party to the dispute or of the Contracting State whose national is a party to the dispute. Annulment: Article 52(3) On receipt of the request [for annulment] the Chairman shall forthwith appoint from the Panel of Arbitrators an *ad hoc* Committee of three persons.[a]	Article 39: The majority of the arbitrators shall be nationals of States other than the Contracting State party to the dispute and the Contracting State whose national is a party to the dispute; provided, however, that the foregoing provisions of this Article shall not apply if the sole arbitrator or each individual member of the Tribunal has been appointed by agreement of the parties. Article 40: (1) Arbitrators may be appointed from outside the Panel of Arbitrators, except in the case of appointments by the Chairman pursuant to Article 38. (2) Arbitrators appointed from outside the Panel of Arbitrators shall possess the qualities stated in paragraph (1) of Article 14. Article 14: (1) Persons designated to serve on the Panels shall be persons of high moral character and recognized competence in the fields of law, commerce, industry or finance, who may be relied upon to exercise independent judgment. Competence in the field of law shall be of particular importance in the case of persons on the Panel of Arbitrators. Annulment: Art. 52 "None of the members of the Committee shall have been a member of the Tribunal which rendered the award, shall be of the same nationality as any such member, shall

TABLE 2 Selection of arbitrators: Rules & obligations of appointing authorities (*cont.*)

Institution	Rules	Requirements
		be a national of the State party to the dispute or of the State whose national is a party to the dispute, shall have been designated to the Panel of Arbitrators by either of those States, or shall have acted as a conciliator in the same dispute."[b]
UNCITRAL	Article 6: 1. Unless the parties have already agreed on the choice of an appointing authority, a party may at any time propose the name or names of one or more institutions or persons, including the Secretary-General PCA, one of whom would serve as appointing authority. 2. If all parties have not agreed on the choice of an appointing authority within 30 days after a proposal made in accordance with paragraph 1 has been received by all other parties, any party may request the Secretary-General of the PCA to designate the appointing authority. 3. Where these Rules provide for a period of time within which a party must refer a matter to an appointing authority and no appointing authority has been agreed on or designated, the period is suspended from the date on which a party initiates the procedure for agreeing on or designating an appointing authority until the date of such agreement or designation. 4. Except as referred to in article 41(4) [reviewing of arbitration fees] if the appointing authority refuses to act, or if it fails to appoint an arbitrator	Article 6: 5. In exercising their functions under these Rules, the appointing authority and the Secretary-General of the PCA may require from any party and the arbitrators the information they deem necessary and they shall give the parties and, where appropriate, the arbitrators an opportunity to present their views in any manner they consider appropriate. All such communications to and from the appointing authority and the Secretary-General of the PCA shall also be provided by the sender to all other parties. 6. When the appointing authority is requested to appoint an arbitrator pursuant to articles 8, 9, 10 or 14, the party making the request shall send to the appointing authority copies of the notice of arbitration and, if it exists, any response to the notice of arbitration. 7. The appointing authority shall have regard to such considerations as are likely to secure the appointment of an independent and impartial arbitrator and shall take into account the advisability of appointing an arbitrator of a nationality other than the nationalities of the parties.

TABLE 2 Selection of arbitrators: Rules & obligations of appointing authorities (*cont.*)

stitution	Rules	Requirements
	within 30 days after it receives a party's request to do so, fails to act within any other period provided by these Rules, or fails to decide on a challenge to an arbitrator within a reasonable time after receiving a party's request to do so, any party may request the Secretary-General of the PCA to designate a substitute appointing authority.	
A bitration les (2012)[c]	Article 7 2. [...] if no other parties have responded to a party's proposal to appoint a sole arbitrator within the time limit provided [...] and the party or parties concerned have failed to appoint a second arbitrator in accordance with articles 9 or 10, the appointing authority may, at the request of a party, appoint a sole arbitrator pursuant to the procedure provided for in article 8, paragraph 2 if it determines that, in view of the circumstances of the case, this is more appropriate. Article 8 1. If the parties have agreed that a sole arbitrator is to be appointed and if within 30 days after receipt by all other parties of a proposal of an individual who would serve as a sole arbitrator the parties have not reached agreement thereon, a sole arbitrator shall, at the request of a party, be appointed by the appointing authority. Article 9: when the parties agreed on three or five arbitrators: If within 30 days after the receipt of a party's	Article 6. 1. The Secretary-General of the Permanent Court of Arbitration shall serve as appointing authority. 2. In exercising its functions under these Rules, the appointing authority may require from any party and the arbitrators the information it deems necessary and it shall give the parties and, where appropriate, the arbitrators, an opportunity to present their views in any manner it considers appropriate. 3. The appointing authority shall have regard to such considerations as are likely to secure the appointment of an independent and impartial arbitrator and shall take into account the advisability of appointing an arbitrator of a nationality other than the nationalities of the parties. Art. 8: 2.The appointing authority shall appoint the sole arbitrator as promptly as possible. In making the appointment, the appointing authority shall use the following list-procedure, unless the parties agree that the list-procedure should not be used or unless the appointing authority determines in its discretion that

TABLE 2 Selection of arbitrators: Rules & obligations of appointing authorities (*cont.*)

Institution	Rules	Requirements
	notification of the appointment of an arbitrator the other party has not notified the first party of the arbitrator it has appointed, the first party may request the appointing authority to appoint the second arbitrator. If within 30 days after the appointment of the second arbitrator, or such other period as may be set by the International Bureau, the two arbitrators have not agreed on the choice of the remaining arbitrators and/or the presiding arbitrator, the remaining arbitrators and/or the presiding arbitrator shall be appointed by the appointing authority in the same way as a sole arbitrator would be appointed under article 8, paragraph 2. Article 10: where three or five arbitrators are to be appointed and there are multiple parties as claimant or as respondent, unless the parties have agreed to another method of appointment of arbitrators, the multiple parties jointly, whether as claimant or as respondent, shall appoint an arbitrator. If the parties have agreed that the arbitral tribunal is to be composed of a number of arbitrators other than one, three, or five, the arbitrators shall be appointed according to the method agreed upon by the parties.	the use of the list-procedure is not appropriate for the case: (a) The appointing authority shall communicate to ea of the parties an identical list containi at least three names; (b) Within 15 day after the receipt of this list, or such oth period as may be set by the Internatio Bureau, each party may return the list the appointing authority, without copy ing the other party, after having delete the name or names to which it objects and numbered the remaining names on the list in the order of its preferenc (c) After the expiration of the above period of time the appointing authori shall appoint the sole arbitrator from among the names approved on the list returned to it and in accordance with the order of preference indicated by th parties; (d) If for any reason the appoi ment cannot be made according to th procedure, the appointing authority m exercise its discretion in appointing th sole arbitrator.

TABLE 2 Selection of arbitrators: Rules & obligations of appointing authorities (*cont.*)

nstitution	Rules	Requirements
	In the event of any failure to constitute the arbitral tribunal under these Rules, the appointing authority shall, at the request of any party, constitute the arbitral tribunal and, in doing so, may revoke any appointment already made and appoint each of the arbitrators and designate one of them as the presiding arbitrator. The appointing authority may, if it deems it appropriate, reappoint previous appointees.	
CC	Art. 12: 2) Where the parties have not agreed upon the number of arbitrators, the Court shall appoint a sole arbitrator, save where it appears to the Court that the dispute is such as to warrant the appointment of three arbitrators. In such case, the claimant shall nominate an arbitrator within a period of 15 days from the receipt of the notification of the decision of the Court, and the respondent shall nominate an arbitrator within a period of 15 days from the receipt of the notification of the nomination made by the claimant. If a party fails to nominate an arbitrator, the appointment shall be made by the Court. 3) […] If the parties fail to nominate a sole arbitrator within 30 days from the date when the claimant's Request for Arbitration has been received by the other party, or within such additional time as may be allowed by the Secretariat, the sole arbitrator shall be appointed by the Court.	Art. 13 1) In confirming or appointing arbitrators, the Court shall consider the prospective arbitrator's nationality, residence and other relationships with the countries of which the parties or the other arbitrators are nationals and the prospective arbitrator's availability and ability to conduct the arbitration in accordance with the Rules. The same shall apply where the Secretary General confirms arbitrators pursuant to Article 13(2). 2) The Secretary General may confirm as co-arbitrators, sole arbitrators and presidents of arbitral tribunals persons nominated by the parties or pursuant to their particular agreements, provided that the statement they have submitted contains no qualification regarding impartiality or independence or that a qualified statement regarding impartiality or independence has not given rise to objections. Such confirmation shall be reported to the Court at its next session. If the Secretary General considers that a

TABLE 2 Selection of arbitrators: Rules & obligations of appointing authorities (*cont.*)

Institution	Rules	Requirements
	4) Three Arbitrators [...] If a party fails to nominate an arbitrator, the appointment shall be made by the Court. 5) Where the dispute is to be referred to three arbitrators, the third arbitrator, who will act as president of the arbitral tribunal, shall be appointed by the Court, unless the parties have agreed upon another procedure for such appointment, in which case the nomination will be subject to confirmation pursuant to Article 13. Should such procedure not result in a nomination within 30 days from the confirmation or appointment of the co-arbitrators or any other time limit agreed by the parties or fixed by the Court, the third arbitrator shall be appointed by the Court. 8) In the absence of a joint nomination pursuant to Articles 12(6) or 12(7) [multiple claimants and respondents] and where all parties are unable to agree to a method for the constitution of the arbitral tribunal, the Court may appoint each member of the arbitral tribunal and shall designate one of them to act as president. In such case, the Court shall be at liberty to choose any person it regards as suitable to act as arbitrator, applying Article 13 when it considers this appropriate.	co-arbitrator, sole arbitrator or preside of an arbitral tribunal should not be cc firmed, the matter shall be submitted t the Court. 3) Where the Court is to appoint an arbitrator, it shall make the appointme upon proposal of a National Committe or Group of the ICC that it considers to be appropriate. If the Court does not accept the proposal made, or if the National Committee or Group fails to make the proposal requested within th time limit fixed by the Court, the Cour may repeat its request, request a proposal from another National Committe or Group that it considers to be appropriate, or appoint directly any person whom it regards as suitable. 4) The Court may also appoint directly to act as arbitrator any person whom i regards as suitable where: a) one or more of the parties is a state may be considered to be a state entity; b) the Court considers that it would be appropriate to appoint an arbitrator from a country or territory where there is no National Committee or Group; or c) the President certifies to the Court that circumstances exist which, in the President's opinion, make a direct appointment necessary and appropriate 5) The sole arbitrator or the president of the arbitral tribunal shall be of a nationality other than those of the partie However, in suitable circumstances ar provided that none of the parties obje

TABLE 2 Selection of arbitrators: Rules & obligations of appointing authorities (*cont.*)

stitution	Rules	Requirements
		within the time limit fixed by the Court, the sole arbitrator or the president of the arbitral tribunal may be chosen from a country of which any of the parties is a national.
'C	Article 17: (2) Where the parties have not agreed on a procedure, or if the Arbitral Tribunal has not been appointed within the time period agreed by the parties or, where the parties have not agreed on a time period, within the time period set by the Board, the appointment shall be made pursuant to paragraphs (3)–(7). (3) Where the Arbitral Tribunal is to consist of a sole arbitrator, the parties shall be given 10 days to jointly appoint the arbitrator. If the parties fail to appoint the arbitrator within this time, the Board shall make the appointment. (4) Where the Arbitral Tribunal is to consist of more than one arbitrator, each party shall appoint an equal number of arbitrators and the Board shall appoint the Chairperson. Where a party fails to appoint arbitrator(s) within the stipulated time period, the Board shall make the appointment. (5) Where there are multiple Claimants or Respondents and the Arbitral Tribunal is to consist of more than one arbitrator, the multiple Claimants, jointly, and the multiple Respondents, jointly, shall appoint an equal number of arbitrators. If either side fails	Article 17(7). When appointing arbitrators, the Board shall consider the nature and circumstances of the dispute, the applicable law, the seat and language of the arbitration and the nationality of the parties.

TABLE 2 Selection of arbitrators: Rules & obligations of appointing authorities (*cont.*)

Institution	Rules	Requirements
	to make such joint appointment, the Board may appoint the entire Arbitral Tribunal.	
LCIA	5.6 The LCIA Court shall appoint the Arbitral Tribunal promptly after receipt by the Registrar of the Response or, if no Response is received, after 35 days from the Commencement Date (or such other lesser or greater period to be determined by the LCIA Court pursuant to Article 22.5). 5.7 No party or third person may appoint any arbitrator under the Arbitration Agreement: the LCIA Court alone is empowered to appoint arbitrators (albeit taking into account any written agreement or joint nomination by the parties). 5.8 A sole arbitrator shall be appointed unless the parties have agreed in writing otherwise or if the LCIA Court determines that in the circumstances a three-member tribunal is appropriate (or, exceptionally, more than three). Article 7: 7.1 If the parties have agreed howsoever that any arbitrator is to be appointed by one or more of them or by any third person (other than the LCIA Court) [...] Such nominee may only be appointed by the LCIA Court as arbitrator subject to that nominee's compliance with Articles 5.3 to 5.5; and the LCIA Court shall refuse to appoint any nominee if it determines that the nominee is not so compliant or is otherwise unsuitable.	5.4 Before appointment by the LCIA Court, each arbitral candidate shall furnish to the Registrar (upon the latte request) a brief written summary of his or her qualifications and professional positions (past and present); the candidate shall also agree in writing fee-rate conforming to the Schedule of Costs; th candidate shall sign a written declaration stating: (i) whether there are any circumstances currently known to the candidate which are likely to give rise i the mind of any party to any justifiable doubts as to his or her impartiality or independence and, if so, specifying in ful such circumstances in the declaration; and (ii) whether the candidate is ready willing and able to devote sufficient time, diligence and industry to ensure the expeditious and efficient conduct of the arbitration. The candidate shall furnish promptly such agreement and declaration to the Registrar. 5.9 The LCIA Court shall appoint arbit tors with due regard for any particular method or criteria of selection agreed in writing by the parties. The LCIA Court shall also take into account the transaction(s) at issue, the nature and circumstances of the dispute, its monetary amount or value, the location an languages of the parties, the number o parties and all other factors which it m consider relevant in the circumstances

TABLE 2 Selection of arbitrators: Rules & obligations of appointing authorities (*cont.*)

stitution	Rules	Requirements
	7.2 Where the parties have howsoever agreed that the claimant or the respondent or any third person (other than the LCIA Court) is to nominate an arbitrator and such nomination is not made within time or at all (in the Request, Response or otherwise), the LCIA Court may appoint an arbitrator notwithstanding any absent or late nomination. Article 8 (Three or More Parties) 8.1 Where the Arbitration Agreement entitles each party howsoever to nominate an arbitrator, the parties to the dispute number more than two and such parties have not all agreed in writing that the disputant parties represent collectively two separate "sides" for the formation of the Arbitral Tribunal (as Claimants on one side and Respondents on the other side, each side nominating a single arbitrator), the LCIA Court shall appoint the Arbitral Tribunal without regard to any party's entitlement or nomination.	5.10 The President of the LCIA Court shall only be eligible to be appointed as an arbitrator if the parties agree in writing to nominate him or her as the sole or presiding arbitrator; and the Vice Presidents of the LCIA Court and the Chairman of the LCIA Board of Directors (the latter being ex officio a member of the LCIA Court) shall only be eligible to be appointed as arbitrators if nominated in writing by a party or parties—provided that no such nominee shall have taken or shall take thereafter any part in any function of the LCIA Court or LCIA relating to such arbitration.

ICSID Convention, Art. 52(3).
ICSID Convention, Art. 52(3).
PCA Arbitration Rules (2012).

TABLE 3 Requirements for arbitration appointment per applicable rules

Institution/ Requirement	ICSID	UNCITRAL
Rules on Nationality	The arbitrators shall be nationals of States other than nationality of either party to the dispute; unless, if the sole arbitrator or each individual member of the tribunal has been appointed by agreement of the parties.[a]	"take into account the advisability of appointing ar arbitrator of a nationality ot than the nationalities of the parties."[b]

	LCIA	ICC
parties are of ent nationalities, le arbitrator or hairperson of bitral Tribunal e of a different ality than the s, unless the s have agreed wise or the Board s it appropriate.[c]	Where the parties are of different nationalities a sole arbitrator or the presiding arbitrator shall not have the same nationality as any party unless the parties who are not of the same nationality as the arbitral candidate all agree in writing otherwise.[d] The nationality of a party shall be understood to include those of its controlling shareholders or interests.[e] A person who is a citizen of two or more States shall be treated as a national of each State; citizens of the European Union shall be treated as nationals of its different Member States and shall not be treated as having the same nationality; a citizen of a state's overseas territory shall be treated as a national of that territory and not of that state; and a legal person incorporated in a state's overseas territory shall be treated as such and not (by such fact alone) as a national of or a legal person incorporated in that state.[f]	In confirming or appointing arbitrators, the Court shall consider the prospective arbitrator's nationality, residence and other relationships with the countries of which the parties or the other arbitrators are nationals and the prospective arbitrator's availability and ability to conduct the arbitration in accordance with the Rules. The same shall apply where the Secretary General confirms arbitrators pursuant to Article 13(2).[g] The sole arbitrator or the president of the arbitral tribunal shall be of a nationality other than those of the parties. However, in suitable circumstances and provided that none of the parties objects within the time limit fixed by the Court, the sole arbitrator or the president of the arbitral tribunal may be chosen from a country of which any of the parties is a national.[h]

TABLE 3 Requirements for arbitration appointment per applicable rules (*cont.*)

Institution/ Requirement	ICSID	UNCITRAL
Rules on Impartiality and Independence	"Persons designated to serve on the Panels shall be person who … may be relied upon to exercise independent judgment."[i]	"The appointing authority shall have regard to such considerations as are likely t[o] secure the appointment of a[n] independent and impartial arbitrator …"[j]
Other Requirements	High moral character and recognized competence in the fields of law, commerce, industry or finance, who may be relied upon to exercise independent judgment. Competence in the field of law shall be of particular importance in the case of persons on the Panel of Arbitrators.[n]	

a ICSID Rules, Art. 39.
b UNCITRAL Arbitration Rules Art. 6(7).
c SCC Arbitration Rules Art. 17(6).
d LCIA Arbitration Rules Art. 6(1).
e LCIA Arbitration Rules Art. 6(2).
f LCIA Arbitration Rules Art. 6(3).
g ICC Arbitration Rules Art 13(1).
h ICC Arbitration Rules Art 13(5).
i ICSID Rules, Art. 14(1).

	LCIA	ICC
arbitrator must partial and endent.[k]	All arbitrators shall be and remain at all times impartial and independent of the parties; and none shall act in the arbitration as advocate for or representative of any party. No arbitrator shall advise any party on the parties' dispute or the outcome of the arbitration.[l]	The Secretary General may confirm as co-arbitrators, sole arbitrators and presidents of arbitral tribunals persons nominated by the parties or pursuant to their particular agreements, provided that the statement they have submitted contains no qualification regarding impartiality or independence or that a qualified statement regarding impartiality or independence has not given rise to objections.[m]
	Before appointment by the LCIA Court, each arbitral candidate shall furnish to the Registrar (upon the latter's request) a brief written summary of his or her qualifications and professional positions (past and present)[o] The LCIA Court shall appoint arbitrators with due regard for any particular method or criteria of selection agreed in writing by the parties.[p]	In confirming or appointing arbitrators, the Court shall consider the prospective arbitrator's nationality, residence and other relationships with the countries of which the parties or the other arbitrators are nationals and the prospective arbitrator's availability and ability to conduct the arbitration in accordance with the Rules.[q]

j UNCITRAL Arbitration Rules Art. 6(7).
k SCC Arbitration Rules Art. 18(1).
l LCIA Arbitration Rules Art. 5(3).
m ICC Arbitration Rules Art 13(2).
n ICSID Rules, Art. 14(1).
o LCIA Arbitration Rules Art. 5(4).
p LCIA Arbitration Rules Art. 5(9).
q ICC Rules, Art. 13(1).

TABLE 4 Summary of challenges procedures

Rules	To whom to file the request?	When to submit?	Who decides?	Reasons for proposal
ICSID	Secretary General	"Promptly" and in any case before the proceedings is declared closed.	The remaining members of the Tribunal if only one arbitrator is challenged. The Chairman of the AC if the remaining members are equally divided or if the proposal refers to the majority or sole arbitrator.	Art. 57 - on account of any fact indicating a manifest lack of the qualities required to be nominated.
UNCITRAL	Communicated directly to the other party, the arbitrator who is challenged, and to the other arbitrators.	Fifteen days after the party has been notified of the appointment of the arbitrator or within fifteen days after learning of the circumstances giving rise to the challenge	If, within fifteen days from the date of the notice, the parties have not agreed on the challenge or the challenged arbitrator has not withdrawn, the party making the challenge may pursue the challenge by seeking, within thirty days from the date of the challenge notice, a decision on the challenge from the appointing authority.	UNCITRAL Rules (2010) Art. 12(1) 1. Any arbitrator may be challenged if circumstances exist that give rise to justifiable doubts as to the arbitrator's impartiality or independence.
ICC	Must be filed with the Secretariat in writing specifying the facts and circumstances on which the challenge is based.	Challenges must be made within thirty days from the appointment or confirmation of the arbitrator, or from the	ICC Court rules on the admissibility and, at the same time, if necessary, on the merits of a challenge	For an alleged lack of impartiality or independence, or otherwise

TABLE 4 Summary of challenges procedures (*cont.*)

les	To whom to file the request?	When to submit?	Who decides?	Reasons for proposal
		date when the party making the challenge was informed of the facts and circumstances.		
C	In writing to the Secretariat.	Within fifteen days from when the circumstances became known to the party. A failure to challenge within the allotted time constitutes a waiver of the right to make the challenge.	If the other party agrees on the challenge, the arbitrator must resign. Otherwise, the Board of Directors of the SCC Arbitration Institute makes the final decision on the challenge	If there are circumstances which "give rise to justifiable doubts as to the arbitrator's impartiality or independence" or if the arbitrator does not possess the qualifications agreed by the parties
A	Submit a written statement to the LCIA Court, the Arbitral Tribunal and all other parties.	Within 14 days of the formation of the Arbitral Tribunal or (if later) within 14 days of becoming aware of any ground	LCIA Court	LCIA Arbitration Rules Article 10.1 if: (i) that arbitrator gives written notice to the LCIA Court of his or her intent to resign as arbitrator, to be copied to all parties and all other members of the Arbitral Tribunal (if any); (ii) that arbitrator falls seriously ill, refuses or becomes unable or unfit to act; or (iii) circumstances exist that give rise to justifiable doubts as to that

TABLE 4 Summary of challenges procedures (*cont.*)

Rules	To whom to file the request?	When to submit?	Who decides?	Reasons for proposal
				arbitrator's impartiali or independence. Or if the arbitrator is unfit under LCIA Arbitration Rules Arti 10.2 if that arbitrator: acts in deliberate viol tion of the Arbitratior Agreement; (ii) does r act fairly or impartiall as between the partie or (iii) does not cond or participate in the arbitration with reaso able efficiency, diliger and industry.

Bibliography

Articles

Bishop, R. Doak & Lucy Reed, *Practical Guidelines for Interviewing, Selecting and Challenging Party-Appointed Arbitrators in International Commercial Arbitration*, 14 Arb. Int'l. 395 (1998).

Bottini, Gabriel, *Should Arbitrator Live on Mars—Challenge of Arbitrators in Investment Arbitration*, 32 Suffolk Transnat'l L. Rev. 341 (2009).

Brower, Charles N.; Stephen W. Schill, *Is Arbitration a Threat or a Boom to the Legitimacy of International Investment Law*, 9 Chi. J. Int'l L. 471 (2009).

Crawford, James, *Treaty and Contract in Investment Arbitration*, 24 Arb. Int'l. 351 (2007).

Douglas, Zachary, *The Hybrid Foundations of Investment Treaty Arbitration*, 2003 Brit. Y.B. Int'l. L. 151 (2004).

Franck, Thomas, *Legitimacy in the International System*, 82 Am. J. Int'l. L. 705 (1988).

Giorgetti, Chiara, *Who Decides Who Decides in International Investment Arbitration?*, 35 U. PA. J. Intl. L. 101 (2014).

Giorgetti, Chiara, *Between Legitimacy and Control: Challenges and Recusals of Arbitrators and Judges in International Courts and Tribunals*, 49 George Washington International Law Review 101 (2016).

Giorgetti, Chiara, *Challenges of International Investment Arbitrators: How Does it Work And Does it Work?* 2 World Arb. And Med. Rev. 2013.

Grossman, Nienke, *The Normative Legitimacy of International Courts*, 86 Temple L. Rev. 61 (2013).

Grossman, Nienke, *Shattering the Glass Ceiling in International Adjudication*, 56 Va. J. Int'l L. 339 (2016).

Grossman, Nienke, *Achieving Sex Representative International Court Benches*, 110 Am. J. Int'l L. 82 (2016).

Langford, Malcolm, Daniel Behn and Runar Hilleren Lie, *The Revolving Door in International Investment Arbitration*, 20 Journal of International Economic Law 301 (2017).

Legum, Barton, *The Innovation of Investor-State Arbitration Under NAFTA*, 43 Harv. J. Int'l. L. 531 (2002).

Lowenfeld, Andreas F., *The Party-Appointed Arbitrator in International Controversies: Some Reflections*, 30 Tex. Int'l L. J. 59 (1995).

Miles, Wendy, *International Arbitrator Appointment*, 57 Dispute Resolution Journal 36 (2002).

Obadia, Eloïse M., *Remarks at 105th ASIL Annual Meeting*, 105 ASIL Ann. Mtg. Proc. 74 (2011).

Partasides, Constantine, *The Selection, Appointment and Challenge of Arbitrators*, 5 Vindabona J. 217 (2001).

Paulsson, Jan, *Arbitration Without Privity*, 10 ICSID Rev. Foreign Investment Law Journal 232 (1995).

Puig, Sergio, *Social Capital in the Arbitration Market*, 25 E. J. Int'l L. 387 (2014).

Puig, Sergio & Gregory Shaffer, *Imperfect Alternatives: Institutional Choice and the Reform of Investment Law*, 112 Am. J. Int'l. L. 361 (2018).

Reisman, W. Michael, *International Arbitration and Sovereignty*, 18 Arb. Int'l. 231 (2002).

Roberts, Anthea, *Clash of Paradigms: Actors and Analogies Shaping the Investment Treaty System*, 107 Am. J. Int'l L. 45 (2012).

Roberts, Anthea, *Incremental, Systemic, and Paradigmatic Reform of Investor-State Arbitration*, 112 Am. J. Int'l L. 410.

Rogers, Catherine, *The Vocation of International Arbitrators*, 20 Am. U. Int'l L. Rev. 958 (2005).

Salomon, Claudia T., *Selecting an International Arbitrator: Five Factors to Consider*, 17 Mealey's Int'l. Arb. Rep. 25 (2002).

Schreuer, Christoph, *The Development of International Law by ICSID Tribunals*, 31(3) Foreign Investment Law Journal 728 (2016).

Smutny, Abby Cohen, *ICSID Arbitration: Procedural Review*, 2 Transnat'l Disp. MGMT 35 (2005).

Swigart, Leigh, *National Judge: Some Reflections on Diversity in International Courts and Tribunals*, 42 McGeorge L. Rev. 224 (2010).

Waibel, Michael & Yanhui Wu, *Are Arbitrators Political?*, ASIL Research Forum 13 (Nov. 5, 2011).

Wangelin, James, *Effective Selection of Arbitrators in International Arbitration*, 14 Mealey's Int'l Arb. Rep. 69 (1999).

Books

Born, Gary B., *International Arbitration: Law and Practice* (Wolters Kluwer, 2012).

Challenges and Recusals of Judges and Arbitrators in International Courts and Tribunals (Chiara Giorgetti ed.) (Brill Nihoff, 2015).

Cleis, Maria Nicole, *The Independence and Impartiality of ICSID Arbitrators: Current Case Law, Alternative Approaches, and Improvement Suggestions* (Brill, 2017).

Daele, Karel, *Challenge and Disqualification of Arbitrators in International Arbitration* (Wolters Kluwer, 2012).

Douglas, Zachary, *The International Law of Investment Claims* (Cambridge University Press, 2009).

Giorgetti, Chiara, *The Arbitral Tribunal: Selection and Replacement of Arbitrators*, in Litigating International Investments Disputes (Chiara Giorgetti ed.) (Nijhoff /Brill Publisher, 2014).

Investment and Commercial Arbitration: Similarities and Divergences (Christina Knahr, Christian Koller, Walter Rechberger & August Reinisch eds.) (Eleven International Publishing, 2009).

Kinnear, Meg et. al., *Building International Investment Law: The First 50 Years of ICSID* (Wolters Kluwer, 2016).

Litigating International Investment Disputes (Chiara Giorgetti ed.) (Martinus Nijhoff, 2014).

Looking to the Future: Essays on International Law in Honor of W. Michael Reisman (Mahnoush H. Arsanjani, Jacob Katz Cogan, Robert D. Sloane, and Siegfried Wiessnereds.) (Martinjus Nihoff, 2010).

Mackenzie, Ruth, et al., *Selecting International Judges- Principles, Process, and Politics* (Oxford University Press 2010).

Practicing Virtue: Inside International Arbitration (David D. Caron, Stephan W. Schill, Abby Cohen Smutny, and Epaminontas E. Triantafilou, eds.) (Oxford University Press, 2015).

Redfern, Alan, Martin Hunter, Nigel Blackaby & Constantine Partasides, *Redfern and Hunter on Arbitration* (Oxford University Press, 2009).

Reed, Lucy, Jan Paulsson & Nigel Blackaby, *Guide to ICSID Arbitration* (Kluwer Law International 2010).

Schreuer, Christopher et al., *The ICSID Convention—A Commentary* (Cambridge University Press, 2009).

Schreuer, Christopher and Rudolph Dolzer, *Principles of International Investment Law* (Oxford University Press, 2008).

St. John, Taylor, *The Rise of Investor-State Arbitration* (Oxford University Press, 2018).

The Rules, Practice, and Jurisprudence of International Courts and Tribunals (Chiara Giorgetti ed.) (Nijhoff /Brill Publisher 2012).

The Iran-United States Claims Tribunal and the Process of International Claims (David Caron and John Crook eds.) (Brill, 2000).

The Oxford Handbook of International Investment Law (P. Muchlinski et al. eds.) (Oxford University Press, 2008).

The Backlash Against Investment Arbitration: Perceptions and Reality (Michael Waibel, Asha Kaushal, Kyo-Hwa Chung and Claire Balchin eds.) (Kluwer Law International, 2010).

www.ingramcontent.com/pod-product-compliance
Lightning Source LLC
Chambersburg PA
CBHW031330230926
51848CB00001B/175
9789004416222